Jesus Christ

Jesus Christ
The Message of the Gospels, the Hope of the Church

BURTON H. THROCKMORTON, JR.

Westminster John Knox Press
Louisville, Kentucky

Scripture quotations from the New Revised Standard Version
of the Bible are copyright © 1989 by the Division of Christian Education
of the National Council of the Churches of Christ in the U.S.A.
All rights reserved. Used by permission.

"Mass for the Day of St. Thomas Didymus, ii. Gloria" by Denise Levertov,
from *Candles in Babylon*. Copyright ©1982 by Denise Levertov.
Reprinted by permission of New Directions Publishing Corp.

"Exodus" by Marge Piercy. Copyright ©1974, 1978 by Marge Piercy and
Middlemarsh, Inc. From *The Twelve-Spoked Wheel Flashing*, published by
Alfred A. Knopf, Inc. Used by permission of the Wallace Literary Agency, Inc.

"The Assumption of Moses," trans. R. H. Charles and rev. J.M.P. Sweet, in
The Apocryphal Old Testament, ed. H.F.D. Sparks (Oxford: Clarendon Press,
1984). Reprinted by permission of Oxford University Press.

Book design by Jennifer K. Cox
Cover design by Kevin Darst

First edition
Published by Westminster John Knox Press
Louisville, Kentucky

This book is printed on acid-free paper that meets the
American National Standards Institute Z39.48 standard. ∞

PRINTED IN THE UNITED STATES OF AMERICA
98 99 00 01 02 03 04 05 06 07 — 10 9 8 7 6 5 4 3 2 1

Library of Congress Cataloging-in-Publication Data

Throckmorton, Burton Hamilton, Jr. 1921–
Jesus Christ : the message of the Gospels, the hope of the church
/ Burton H. Throckmorton. — 1st ed.
          p.   cm.
Includes bibliographical references and indexes.
ISBN 0-664-25735-6 (alk. paper)
1. Jesus Christ—Person and offices—Biblical teaching.   2. Bible.
N.T. Gospels—Theology.   3. Bible. N.T. Gospels—Hermeneutics.
4. Jesus Christ—Historicity.   I. Title.
BT205.T55   1998
232—dc21   97-47501

For
Joan Barrows Throckmorton Simmons,
my sister and lifelong friend

CONTENTS

Preface   ix

1. Multiple Testimonies   1
2. Difficulties in Discovering Jesus   18
3. Gospel Sources and Texts   24
4. The Dominion of God   40
5. The Hermeneutics of Rudolf Bultmann   53
6. Before Hermeneutics   59
7. Metaphor   67
8. Signs, Images, and Symbols   74
9. Myth, Symbol, and Dominion of God   81
10. Signs in Mark of the Dominion of God   92
11. The Dominion of God Today   100
12. Jesus and the Law   107
13. Jesus' Resurrection   119
Epilogue   132

Notes   137

Index of Biblical References   142
Index of Names   144

PREFACE

In a recent brochure publicizing works on Jesus, the front page has photographs of the jackets of seven recent books, and in large print at the top we read: "Searching for the Historical Jesus." Underneath that, a question is asked: "As Christianity Approaches the 21st Century, Which Portrait of JESUS Will Emerge as the Definitive One?" What in the world are we coming to when that question can be asked seriously by a reputable publisher? Which recently published book on who Jesus was will prove to be *definitive*? What is a definitive "life of Jesus"? Are the Gospels no longer in the running here? I am expecting any day to be informed by some advertiser that I can find the real Jesus on the Internet, and I can put the Gospels to one side for a less complicated and more modern figure. The commercialization of books about Jesus is tending toward the vulgar. We are told in so many words by one publisher after another that the author of the book it has published has finally fathomed the mystery of who the *real* Jesus actually was, and that if you buy its book you can at last "read all about him." Finally, as we move into the twenty-first century, the secret has been unlocked, the mystery of who the one is who was "*with* God," who "*was* God," and who "became flesh and lived among us" (John 1:1, 14). The one who is "the bread of God" that "comes down from heaven and gives life to the world" (John 6:33), and who gives the "living water" to those who know "the gift of God" (John 4:10), turns out to be a cardboard abstraction, an image of the archaeologist who thinks he or she has at last discovered the lost Jesus. There is more mystery in every person I know than there is in recent portraits found in the "top ten" books on Jesus. If Susan Sontag is right that "interpretation is the revenge of the mind on art," then it may be that these recent "biographies" of Jesus are the revenge of scholars on the Gospels.

The assurance with which writers have sketched out the person of Jesus with a few strokes of carefully selected words taken from the Gospels, supplemented by a few other words picked up from non-Gospel sources, with the purpose, apparently, of displacing almost all of the great variety of New Testament witnesses, would be unbelievable if it were not so concretely manifested. What function do the Gospels serve in the church if they are not credible witnesses, but rather grossly distort the person of Jesus? Can a person know Jesus by reading any one of these books, or all of them? Manifestly not; but we are not usually advised by these authors that reading the Gospels might be illuminating in even a supplementary way.

In any case, from where I sit the question of who the Sovereign of the church was and is, of who the one who is repeatedly preached in the church is, has been badly obscured, and many answers given to the question have been highly deceptive and misleading. Recently, in 1996, Luke Timothy Johnson published a work (*The Real Jesus*) that was very critical of this recent barrage of books about Jesus, and of the fact that "this sort of ersatz scholarship was being taken for the real thing."[1] Johnson exposed book after book for what it was, but I am not sure how convincing he was to the "Jesus scholars" and their hangers-on, who will not be easily or quickly dissuaded from their idiosyncratic views. In this book I am not going to engage these recent authors in debate. I think the whole "Jesus movement" is too far off the point, too esoteric, too confined to a very small group of New Testament scholars, and simply too irrelevant to the life and faith of the church for one to be able to contribute anything productive in response to it; and Luke Johnson has already done, so very well, what might be done.

A recent article in the *New York Times* (November 25, 1996) has informed us that Robert W. Funk, the founder of the "Jesus

Preface

Seminar," is launching out in a new direction. Not satisfied to have stated his conclusion that "eighty-two percent of the words ascribed to Jesus in the gospels were not actually spoken by him,"[2] he now wants to further obscure the relevance of the Bible in the church by altering its canon. If you can't make Jesus say all the things you want him to say by tampering with the Gospels, the next move would be to make some additions to the Gospels that *will* say just what you think Jesus ought to have said. That is also the way to create a new church, whose canon is no longer what it finally became after 400 years of history in the church, but is "my own canon." The creation of a new "church" would be the last stop of the bus.

There is nothing wrong with any scholars, who have the interest, voting which words of the Gospels they think Jesus most likely spoke, and there is nothing wrong in speculating that on occasion a non-Gospel source will contain a form of a saying closer to what Jesus probably said than the form it takes in our Gospels. None of this is new. What is to be objected to, however, is the dogmatic way in which the conclusions of the recent "Jesus scholars" have been presented, the impression created by the multiplicity of their publications that these conclusions are practically irrefutable, and the implication that other scholars' work is simply passé.

This book is written to say something very different from what the current tide is producing about who the Jesus is who is attested in the Gospels. It is far less negative about the witness of the Gospels, and far more affirming about their place in the life of faith. All historical scholars who study the Gospels ask basic historical and literary questions about them; but answers to these questions need not be offered to displace the Gospels themselves. I will ask many of these same questions, questions that are generally asked by scholars, and that lay people should also be encouraged to ask. But this book is written to *illuminate* the Gospels, not to displace them, not to find a Jesus who is quite different from the figure portrayed in the New Testament. It is written to keep active, inquiring church members abreast of the kinds of questions that are regularly asked in seminaries and theological schools.

Preface

As I lecture to many different audiences I am repeatedly told by lay people that their ministers have not been informing them about what they need to know to read the New Testament intelligently, that they are, in fact, withholding from them what they learned in theological school. Often these lay people are very well educated, except when it comes to reading and understanding the Bible. There they are not much different from children, and in fact read the Bible just as they did in Sunday school. There is no reason for such ignorance to exist in the church; in fact, such ignorance of the Bible and how to read it is inexcusable. I hope in this little book to illustrate the kinds of questions one needs to ask when reading the Gospels, and to give some direction in how to look for answers. May this book function as a guide to the Gospels, and into the mystery of one aspect of the teaching of the historical person, Jesus Christ, the church's Sovereign.

[1]

Multiple Testimonies

In the New Testament believers are presented with a great variety of witnesses to who Jesus was. Though one may try to weed through these testimonies to discover what may be called the "real" Jesus, as distinguished from the Jesus portrayed with christological overlays in the New Testament, that real Jesus, one will always discover, proves to be very elusive. But the believer will continue to want to know who that real Jesus was, and will continue to go back to the New Testament to try to find him. John says that the temple police said to the chief priests and Pharisees, "No one has ever spoken like this" (John 7:46).

Matthew tells us that Jesus "taught them as one having authority, and not as their scribes" or anyone else (Matt. 7:29). Over and over again in the Gospels Jesus is said to have *taught*. But what did Jesus teach? What was so remarkable about Jesus' teaching? Was most of what Jesus taught forgotten and lost forever when Jesus was crucified? Are the teachings as represented in the four Gospels almost entirely fabrications of the early church? Or are the testimonies of the Gospels concerning Jesus' words reasonably, or at least partially, correct? Does it make much difference to the church whether or not the Gospels accurately represent what Jesus said?

Recently the well-known "Jesus Seminar" has been investigating the accuracy of the Gospel accounts of what Jesus said, concluding that Jesus said less than a fifth of the words he is represented to have said in our Gospels. This seminar has spawned a spate of "lives of Jesus," each of them representing a point of view quite different from the others. What is the church to make of all this? What are teachers in the church to teach about Jesus? What are ministers to preach? Are there any certainties to undergird one who attempts to proclaim the gospel every week? Or are the sands continually shifting, with one scholar insisting that *these* words represent what Jesus said, and another pointing to quite different words? Does no word of Jesus, or word about Jesus, remain on which one can rely? The questions have profound implications for the life and faith of every believer, and for the church itself.

Let's begin by noting the fact that the church inherited many different testimonies about who Jesus was, what Jesus said, and what he did. From its very beginning the church was founded on the person and work of Jesus Christ, and after the death of the generation of disciples who had known Jesus, the oral tradition about Jesus that the disciples had initiated grew and developed and was passed on to their successors who, in turn, passed it on to others. During this time various developing traditions were "frozen," were written down in the form of "gospels," and four of those gospels were put together early in the second century in the collection that makes up the church's Gospel canon. The oral forms of the "gospel," however, continued to develop and were highly respected until the middle of the second century. Since the middle of the third century, however, the four-Gospel canon has been widely known and used in the church, and ever since then the church has lived with just that collection, though many other gospels were known and read. We should also note here the important but often overlooked fact that the four Gospels acquired their standing as scripture *as a collection,* not individually. No one Gospel has taken precedence over the others, and no one Gospel or selection from the four Gospels has constituted scripture. The church has inherited the testimony of four Gospels — in their entirety — as a unit.

Of course, in addition to the Gospels, the church has still earlier written testimony about Jesus from the apostle Paul, as well as additional witnesses from other New Testament writers. The church is and has always been the community that inherited and preserved multiple testimony to and about the person of Jesus Christ.

Multiple Testimonies

The process of formulating what became the entire New Testament canon extended through four centuries, but with the exception of seven books (three of them not noteworthy for either historical or theological reasons), all the other twenty books were acknowledged as authoritative throughout the church by the end of the second century. What led to the surfacing of just these books as canon? No judgment of bishops, or council of bishops, or pope gave the canon its imprimatur. Those twenty-seven books survived as canon because of the way the canon developed in the church. The canon is simply a record of a major part of what was, as it turned out, the decisive form of the church's own early tradition, the tradition which was to form the church, which developed with the church, and by which the church lived. The authority of the canon is validated by what became its uninterrupted use in the whole church as authoritative. The church did not create or establish the authority of the canon by decree. It was the judgment of the churches that what became the "Gospels and epistles" in their widely circulated manifestations, was to be normative for their life and faith in the same sense as were the "law and the prophets." Tradition preceded scripture, and was and is perpetuated in scripture.

As I have stated in another work, "The authority of the message that these books proclaim did not rest upon a (single) decision of the church that might later be called into question. No, the message witnessed to in these books was the message that had called into being the Christian communities of the Roman Empire. For these communities to question the proclamation of faith that they had received in its written form would have been for them to question the witness they were making in the world and to question the new foundation upon which their lives had been set and in devotion to which not a few lives had been sacrificed."[1]

But this very multiplicity of witnesses, and the diversity of theological points of view they represent, have very often, since very early times, been a source of confusion and embarrassment or regret in the church. There have been those who have sought to reduce the inherited tradition to one or another lowest common denominator. In the second century, Marcion, who rejected entirely the church's scriptures that later became its Old Testament, adopted an abbreviated form of our Gospel of Luke (or a shortened version of it) as his only Gospel, to which he added ten Pauline letters to form his scripture. And in about 170 C.E. Tatian solved the problem created for him by the existence of four Gospels in a different way—he wove together the contents of all four Gospels into a single narrative, a harmonizing of the Gospels, in a work known as the *Diatessaron*. This was Tatian's way of eliminating the problem of multiple Gospel sources. He homogenized the four Gospels into one gospel; but what he produced and handed down was not what the tradition had handed him at all, but was his own new "Tatian gospel," which the church was to reject. The church stood fast in holding that the four Gospels in their entirety constituted the gospel witness to Jesus.

But Marcion and Tatian in the second century were not alone in trying to pare down the multiplicity of witnesses to Christ. As people began to ask critical questions in the eighteenth century, the rise of questions especially about the Gospels, the multiple testimonies to who Jesus was, and what Jesus said and did presented the church with a considerable challenge: How are all the dissimilarities in the Gospel accounts to be synthesized? It was argued that Jesus could not have said contrary things, that he probably did not repeat himself verbatim on several occasions, and that he could not very well have done exactly the same things at different times. In order to deal with these kinds of contradictions, "lives of Jesus" began to appear, and Gospel material was rearranged. The earliest such life was written a little over two hundred years ago by the German scholar Reimarus, the first parts of which were published posthumously by Lessing in 1774 and 1778. Before that time books written about Jesus had principally taken the form of harmonies and paraphrases. From the sixteenth century until the end of the eighteenth, Christians—both Protestants and Catholics—believed that the teaching of Jesus agreed perfectly with the teaching of their respective churches, a view still held by many; they also believed that in the four canonical Gospels they had a very reliable picture of the story of Jesus' life. Nothing more "critical" than that kind of selection and rearrangement was called for until the end of the eighteenth century.

The nineteenth century produced great optimism in the Western world about what could be achieved on all fronts by the human race. History tended to be interpreted by the analogy of people climbing a flight of stairs. They might trip, but their basic movement was from downstairs to upstairs. Herbert Spencer wrote, for instance: "The ultimate development of man is logically certain—as certain as any conclusion in which we place the most implicit faith; for instance, that all men will die."[2] Under the assumption that progress was a necessity, and that historiography was an exact or near-exact science, a number of biographies of Jesus emerged in the Western world, though this productivity petered out in the 1920s.

There were a number of reasons for this: (1) the historians' investigations into Jesus' life did not arrive at the same conclusions—which Jesus was the real Jesus? (2) Jesus "as he really was" was surprisingly nineteenth-centuryish, and markedly Ritschlian in appearance (see pp. 44–45 for a discussion of Ritschl)—there had obviously been a circular reading of the past in terms of the present. Revolutionaries found Jesus to have been a revolutionary, pacifists found Jesus to have been a pacifist, Marxists found him to have been an early Marxist, and ascetics discovered to their surprise that Jesus was just like one of them. (3) This Jesus "as he really was" often did not seem very interesting. It could be, of course, that Jesus had been rather commonplace after all; but it would take more than a few Ph.D.'s in New Testament who disagreed with one another to convince the church of this. The church had known its Sovereign pretty well for a good many centuries, indeed throughout its whole history, without the enlightenment of a single critical "life of Jesus." Perhaps the newly discovered scientific methods of the historiographer were not as yet quite adequate to the task of reproducing the historical person, Jesus, faithfully and in all the dimensions of his historical existence.

The nineteenth-century assumption of the perfectibility of humankind included an assumption of the perfectibility of historiography; but if the former assumption were shaken, then faith in the reliability of historiography would be undermined. Yet the nineteenth century also produced writers who were not heard in their own time and were critical of the common assumptions of their age, but who would prove to be very influential in the next century. Among these major voices were Jacob Burckhardt in Switzerland (1818–97), who denied the "progressive development" of history, and affirmed only a constant flux. In France there were Gustave Flaubert (1821–80) and Charles Baudelaire (1821–67), who, at the age of thirty, wrote: "The world is drawing to a close. Only for one reason can it last longer: just because it happens to exist. . . . I invite any thinking person to show me what is left of life. Religion! It is useless to talk about it, or to look for its remnants; it is a scandal that one takes the trouble even of denying God."[3] In Denmark there was Søren Kierkegaard (1813–55) and in Germany, Friedrich Nietzsche (1844–1900); in Russia there were Fyodor Dostoevsky (1821–81) and Leo Tolstoy (1828–1910)—all of them born in the early part of the nineteenth century. Dostoevsky said that Western civilization, an "ant-hill on a rotten foundation, lacking every universal and absolute, is completely undermined";[4] and Tolstoy wrote: "How easily do individuals as well as whole nations take their own so-called civilization as the true civilization: finishing one's studies, keeping one's nails clean, using the tailor's and the barber's services, travelling abroad, and the most civilized man is complete."[5] So the nineteenth century produced two very different influences—on the one hand, great optimism, and on the other hand, great pessimism about what could be known and achieved.

Furthermore, in addition to the points of view we have noted above, there was also in the nineteenth century another factor that would work against the writing of biographies of Jesus: the development of *historicism,* according to which the subjectivity and value judgments of the historian were, as far as possible, to be eliminated. The purpose of eliminating value judgments was to increase objectivity and so serve the interest of truth. But then how could one say anything about the *significance* of past occurrences if one had refrained from making any value judgments? If, in the interest of objectivity, one will not ask the question of meaning, then the possibility of detecting any meaning in history is relinquished. So historicism led to relativism, and doubts about the meaning of historical data led ultimately, in the case of gospel criticism, to the cessation of the attempt to discover more. The possibility of discovering the real Jesus in the data supplied by the Gospels became highly problematic. Furthermore, in the early twentieth century some important facts about the Gospels themselves were noted. We will mention a few of these very briefly.

Julius Wellhausen in 1906 published his view that the Gospels were primarily sources for the history of the early church, and only secondarily sources for the history of Jesus.[6] He believed that the Gospel narratives could not be taken at face value with regard to determining details about the life of Jesus, and that it was possible to make only some general deductions from them.

Wilhelm Wrede wrote in 1901 that the author of the Gospel of Mark did not write as an objective historian, but as a "theologian" of the "Messianic secret,"[7] thus Wrede held that the earliest Gospel did not provide accurate historical information about Jesus.

Karl Ludwig Schmidt demonstrated in 1919 that the order of events in the Gospels is not based on anyone's memory of the order of Jesus' public ministry, but resulted from a later arrangement of sayings and stories, organized topically or theologically.[8] If all these scholars were right, historians could not very well discover what they were looking for—Jesus "as he really was."

Finally, a new point of view arose that led to the end of the former quest of the historical Jesus. It was that the Gospels are primarily kerygmatic, or preaching material, and only secondarily and indirectly the records of objective facts. So the investigation of the *kerygma*, the preaching of the church—which includes the *significance* of Jesus—began to replace the investigation of the historical facts about Jesus as the focus of study in the early decades of the twentieth century.

Now it must be conceded that all these developments that led to a hiatus in the writing of "lives of Jesus" continue to have force to the present day. Though they no longer forestall the writing of such lives, as the recent appearance of many such volumes demonstrates, in varying degrees they still remain pertinent.

A "new quest" for the historical, or "real," Jesus was begun in 1953 with a now-famous lecture delivered by Ernst Käsemann entitled, "The Problem of the Historical Jesus."[9] That lecture led to the ushering in of new attempts to write lives of Jesus which, as N. T. Wright has observed, have "rumbled on for nearly thirty years without producing much in the way of solid results."[10]

Now we are in the midst of another lively (some would say fruitful) period of the generation of lives of Jesus. The impetus for a great deal of this activity was undoubtedly produced by the work of the American "Jesus Seminar," founded in 1985 by Robert W. Funk. The fruits of conclusions drawn by this seminar have been widely advertised, and are very well known. Regularly active, voting members of the Jesus Seminar, apparently about forty in number, ranked more than 1,500 sayings attributed to Jesus in the four canonical Gospels, plus the noncanonical Gospel of Thomas. Colors were given to four groups of sayings: (1) *red* was given to sayings believed by the members to represent closely what Jesus said; (2) *pink* to sayings about whose authenticity some doubt remained; (3) *grey* to sayings that did not come from Jesus but reflect something close to what Jesus might have said; (4) *black* to sayings that Jesus never uttered, but were either created out of whole cloth by Jesus' followers or were borrowed from common lore. These colors were attributed to each saying by vote of the seminar members. In the book that lays out the work of this seminar, *The Five Gospels,*[11] every saying of the four Gospels is printed in one of the four colors.

When one looks at the Sermon on the Mount in Matthew 5—7, as found in *The Five Gospels,* one is startled to find the results of the polling of the voting members of the Jesus Seminar. According to the members of that panel the following words from those three chapters were probably uttered by Jesus, and are printed in red:

Matt. 5:39–42a
Matt. 5:44 (the words "Love your enemies")
Matt. 6:9 (the two words "Our Father" from Jesus' prayer)

Multiple Testimonies

That is the sum total of the entire collection from Matthew 5—7 of words believed to have been undoubtedly spoken by Jesus. I also count twenty-one verses in the Sermon on the Mount printed in *pink,* representing what Jesus might possibly have said. All the rest of the sermon is printed in grey or black—not thought to have been said by Jesus. So one can see at a glance that according to the Jesus Seminar very little of the Sermon on the Mount sheds light on what Jesus said, and therefore on who Jesus was.

The situation is precisely the same when one looks at the whole Gospel canon. According to the Jesus Seminar the following verses constitute every word from the four Gospels that one may count as an authentic word of Jesus:

> Matt. 5:39–42a = Luke 6:29–30a
>
> Matt. 5:44a = Luke 6:27 (the words "Love your enemies")
>
> Matt. 6:9a = Luke 11:2 (the words "Our Father" from Jesus' prayer). Interestingly, Jesus' Gethsemane prayer to God in Mark 14:36, which begins "Abba, Father," is printed in black—not Jesus' words.
>
> Matt. 13:33 = Luke 13:20–21
>
> Matt. 22:21 = Mark 12:17
>
> Luke 6:20–21
>
> Luke 10:30–35 (Parable of the Good Samaritan)
>
> Luke 16:1–8a (The Unjust Manager)
>
> Matt. 20:1–15 (Parable of the Laborers in the Vineyard)
>
> No words in the Gospel of John are printed in red.

The majority of members of the Jesus Seminar have made public in print their view that only these eight verses in the Gospels, plus two parables and a single story, almost certainly come from Jesus. That is mighty slim pickings. If it were generally agreed that these were in fact the only authentic words we had from Jesus, we could say practically nothing about him at all; we certainly could not write a "life of Jesus," and we could let our imaginations run wild. Clearly the view represented by the seminar is a minority view, but the fact that a majority of the members of this American seminar, made up primarily of New Testament scholars, voted as they did tells us that in their view, for whatever it's worth, the correspondence between words spoken by the real Jesus and words spoken by the Jesus portrayed in the Gospels is practically nil.

It seems clear that there is a negative estimate among members of the Jesus Seminar with regard to the Gospels' accuracy in their representations of Jesus, one not different in kind from early nineteenth-century views on the subject. On the one hand, of course, there are those who believe that what the Gospels say about Jesus is divinely inspired and unquestionably true. But critical studies of the Gospels must deal with the question of sources, their age, and their origin, and all critical lives of Jesus assume judgments made about precisely which words and stories in the Gospels accurately represent, or probably represent, the real Jesus about whom the life is being written. Differences among lives of Jesus reflect differences in those judgments, and one will note that every life of Jesus is very different from every other one.

Characterizations of Jesus have run all the way from the view that Jesus was a magician,[12] to the view that Jesus was a teacher in the Essene community,[13] or that Jesus was a holy man from Galilee,[14] or a rabbi,[15] or a political revolutionary.[16] Recently Jesus has been characterized as a philosopher of the Cynic school.[17] While it is possible to find in the Gospels a trace of evidence that Jesus was a charismatic, or a secret Zealot, or that he occasionally spoke in aphorisms, or that he might be characterized occasionally as having had any one of a number of other interests, none of these charismatic gifts, or aphorisms, or other ways of identifying Jesus would seem to be able to account for the monumental influence of Jesus' life on the community which that life created and, subsequently, for the influence of that life on the world.

We should add that New Testament scholars are not the only people who have written lives of Jesus. The theologian and physician-missionary Albert Schweitzer once said that those who write about Jesus' life wind up by revealing their own true selves. There is surely much truth to that statement. Early in this century the social revolutionary Eugene V. Debs described Jesus as the greatest working-class organizer in history. Later Bruce Barton, an advertising executive, described Jesus in *The Man Nobody Knows: A Discovery of the Real Jesus*[18] as a great entrepreneur whose parables had the effect of good commercial slogans. Recently a book written by Bob Briner, a sports marketer and television producer, explains how the message of the Gospels can work in the corporate world.[19] And so we can say that Jesus, like God, is always turning out to be very much like me.

What is the significance of these differences, of all the variety there is among the "lives" of Jesus? What is the significance of the prior fact that critical studies of the Gospels lead inevitably to the making of distinctions about degrees of accuracy among the many and varied recorded "sayings of Jesus"? The question is of great concern in the church, but it is a complicated question requiring more than one answer. We may note in the first place that the historical question of which, among all the sayings in the Gospels, were really spoken by Jesus is a modern question, not one asked by the church throughout most of its history; but once the question was asked, answers to it had to be sought.

The historical question of sources in the Gospels is the same as the question of the sources of any other historical document, but in the *church* the Gospels are not just mere literature; in the *church* the Gospels—all of the Gospels, not selections from among them—are scripture and canon.

We should note that for the Gospel authors it was the one believed to be Sovereign in the church whose historical life was traced. It was not that the historical details of Jesus' life led to the author's faith that Jesus was Sovereign; it was the other way around—the Sovereign Jesus led believers to inquire into who the *historical* person Jesus was. And this remains true in the church: believers seek to know and understand the historical life of the one who is Sovereign among them.

We have four such "lives" of Jesus in the New Testament, each one very different from the others. And lying behind each of the Gospels are traditions that their authors differently understood and differently interpreted. It is also clear that each of the Gospels contains interpretations of Jesus' words that frequently are presented not as commentary on Jesus' words, but as Jesus' own words; not as coming from the church, but as coming from Jesus. There is, for example, the Marcan addition to Jesus' words, copied by both Matthew and Luke, "so that the Human One is lord even of the sabbath" (Mark 2:28, Inclusive Version).[20] These words are surely Mark's commentary on the preceding words of Jesus, found in Mark 2:27, but they are presented not as written by Mark, but as spoken by Jesus. Critical study of the Bible leads us to this conclusion.

One might also venture the guess that not every Christian would have accepted as authentic or true Mark's addition to Jesus' words, but the canon is the result of a historical development wherein the influence of certain written works prevailed over others. It represents the victory of some Christian parties over others—canonical Gospels over the Gospel of Thomas, for instance.

One could argue that dissenting views that never made it into the formation of the canon are as worthy of affirmation as are canonical views; but the church's life and faith are inextricably tied to its scripture, and not to other writings that did not become canon. To alter the church's canon would be to modify (at the least) or transfigure (at the most) the church into a different institution.

What is the significance for the *church* of these observations? What is the significance, for instance, for the *church* of the evidence that not every word represented in the Gospels as spoken by Jesus was Jesus' word? What is the significance for the *church* of the evidence that our Gospels often represent beliefs that were denied by other Christians? What is the significance for the *church* of the evidence that there are layers of tradition in our Gospels, some much older than others? Do the older traditions carry a weight or authority that is not inherent in later ones? I think there can be no single answer to these questions, because the church includes people of very different interests, interests that may seem to have little in common with each other, but which, in fact, are all clearly related.

We can illustrate these differences by considering the work and interests of the scholar, the preacher, the actively inquiring layper-

—12—

son, and the average believer. These four groups lie on a continuum, but the emphasis of each in relation to the scriptures is quite different. Let us consider them in reverse order.

By the "average believer" I am referring to the person who attends church worship once in a while, who does not go to special services or Bible study classes, and who does not read the Bible at home. Such people have little interest in scripture, and probably make up most of the church membership in what used to be called "mainline churches." For such people the questions asked above about the Gospels are uninteresting and irrelevant.

Second, there are those we might call "actively inquiring lay people." These are active church members who occasionally read scripture at home, who are active participants in Bible study classes when they are offered, and who constitute the vital center and core of every local congregation. For these people the questions asked above are somewhat puzzling, the implications not quite understood. They want to know more about what the questions imply but they find it very difficult to find answers. Many of them are satisfied to read scripture without regard to any of the questions raised, but others remain frustrated at not being able to move ahead in discovering ways to think about such questions and possible answers to them.

In the third place there are the pastors and preachers who—in so-called "liberal" churches—have been exposed to the critical study of the Bible while they were in seminary. A minority of them were Bible majors or serious students of the Bible; others never had a very large interest in historical-critical questions, and never raise such questions in their sermon preparations or sermons. Among these we find a great diversity in interest, in knowledge, in serious Bible study, and in hermeneutical method; but with this group abides the ever-to-be-hoped-for possibility that increasingly critical questions will be asked and given some attention.

In the fourth place there are the biblical scholars whose interest remains centered on answering these and other historical and literary questions. The difference among these four groups of Christians is one of emphasis, running all the way from no interest to primary interest in the study of the Bible, but something more should be said about the work and emphasis of biblical scholars.

Very often scholars in the field of biblical studies center their interests on historical and literary questions, quite aside from the relevance of their work to the life and faith of the contemporary church. Their work may become more and more esoteric—for example, to determine how much gold was sold in Corinth in the year 50 C.E. Such investigations may be important as a basis on which the interpretation of some passage or other can be built by others, but if its significance for any part of the New Testament is not interpreted, it will have no meaning for others in the church. We must maintain the hope that the continuum between the work of the scholar, the work of the preacher, and the concerns of the layperson will be strengthened. This would require a conversation and dialogue that is very largely absent in the church.

Historical and literary criticism are necessary preliminaries to the work of the preacher or the study of the layperson. Because the Gospels (and, indeed, all biblical literature) are culturally conditioned—that is, they were written by human beings who lived in certain times and places—they reflect judgments and values of their own day. To be a slave and to be a slave owner, for example, were common situations in the first century, and so Paul could write, "Were you a slave when called? Do not be concerned about it. Even if you gain your freedom, make use of your present condition now more than ever. . . . In whatever condition you were called, brothers and sisters, there remain with God" (1 Cor. 7:21, 24). Historical criticism investigates the circumstances Paul assumes here, and the preacher can use the critic's work in explaining this past circumstance and in tracing developments that have altered present-day judgments with regard to it. The same is true of innumerable situations that were culturally determined, were taken for granted in the first century, and are reflected in our Gospels. The historical critic will uncover these and so help the preacher, as well as the general believer, to illuminate passages that would otherwise be much more difficult to interpret without the scholars' investigations.

Multiple Testimonies

Once one has been introduced to the critical study of the Gospels, one can never return to a precritical view of them—once one has learned *anything,* there can be no prospect of resuming one's former place. And once one has said "Yes" to the gospel, then the words of the Gospels are heard as scripture, that is, as Word from God.

In their study of the Gospels many scholars have concluded that some of the Gospels' testimony is true, and that the rest is not. They assume that where there is conflicting testimony, the testimony of only one witness is ever true, that the perception of only one witness corresponds to "what actually happened," and that all other perceptions are false. For the past three hundred years or so, except for a noteworthy hiatus after Rudolf Bultmann, scholars have been searching the Gospels to discover words of Jesus, or words about Jesus, that they can announce correspond to what they believe really happened. Their pronouncements remain in some tension with the fact that the variations in the testimonies found in the New Testament have been, and remain, constitutive for the church—that the whole of the text, not just some scholar's summary or condensation of it, is open to be read as scripture. There is always a tension between recognizing that the Gospels are made up of many different sources, and understanding them as scripture. Using historical and literary criticism, one may conclude that Jesus probably said "A," but undoubtedly did not say "B"; but for preaching and evangelism purposes, for purposes of one's own spiritual life, with regard to individual faith, what is the significance of that judgment? While it is true that historical and literary judgments will affect one's understanding and interpretation of a passage, it is also true that both sayings, "A" and "B," are in the canon and both *may* be heard as scripture, as Word from God.

Recent studies of the New Testament have disclosed a multiplicity of theological viewpoints in the canon itself: Jewish Christianity, different sorts of Hellenistic Christianity, Christian apocalypses, and early Catholic Christianity—all of them to be found there. Because of this great variety, it is difficult for the church any longer to think of the whole canon, as a unit, to reflect a single theological norm.[21] This means that discrete sources in the canon must be dealt with separately, not considered to be lesser parts of a single more authoritative entity but as contributing to a compilation of equal units. Many Protestants speak of a "canon within the canon," of a theological quintessence to which the remainder of the canon is related. On the face of it, a "canon within the canon" would seem to be the only way the scriptures can be interpreted, given the fact that the whole of the Bible cannot serve as a theological norm; but, of course, that quintessence will vary with each person who discovers it. Marcion and Tatian tried the way of a "canon within the canon," and the church that survived repudiated both attempts. It appears that the church will not allow any single theological view to be absolutized. Variety among theological stances is inherent in the church. The canon is the repository of the church's earliest tradition, and it is the final canonical form of the text that designates various theological traditions as normative.

One final very important consideration: the New Testament, like the Old Testament, will always be misread so long as it is read and heard as cut-in-stone instruction, with a single, obvious, univocal meaning. Furthermore, every reader must resist the temptation, so far as possible, to manipulate the interpretation of a text; but we must make the same distinction between the "letter" and the "Spirit" that Paul warned the Corinthians to make in their reading and hearing of their (Old Testament) scripture. Paul wrote to the Corinthians that we have been "made worthy to be servants of a new covenant, not of letter but of spirit; for the letter kills, but the Spirit makes alive" (2 Cor. 3:6, author's translation). Paul knew that the Jew could be obedient to the letter of the law, but at the same time could be disobedient to the will of God, while the Gentile, who did not know the law as "letter," could fulfill it. Remember his words to the Romans, "a person is a Jew who is one inwardly, and real circumcision is a matter of the heart—it is spiritual and not literal. Such a person receives praise not from others but from God" (Rom. 2:29).

The Christian is called to "discernment" (cf. 1 Cor. 2:14–15, "those who are spiritual discern all things") and must therefore listen to the scriptures "spiritually," that is, with the aid of the Spirit. The New Testament words are *not* Word from God resting on a page; the New Testament becomes Word from God if it is spiritually discerned—that is, if it is heard as gospel. In his *Lectures on Romans* Martin Luther wrote: "The apostle means by 'letter' not merely those parts of Scripture that have a symbolical significance and the teaching of the law, but, rather, every teaching that prescribes what constitutes the good life whether it is to be found in the Gospel or in Moses. For when one learns it and keeps it in one's memory and the Spirit of grace is not present, it is merely an empty letter and the soul's death."[22]

[2]

Difficulties in Discovering Jesus

In light of the multiple witnesses to Jesus that the church possesses; in light of differing and conflicting statements about what Jesus said and did; and in light also of the variety of ways in which various Gospel authors have interpreted Jesus' words and deeds, how can one sort through it all and hope to arrive at a picture of Jesus that one can believe, with some assurance, corresponds roughly to the historical person of Jesus? How is one to explain the great number of different estimates by New Testament scholars of who Jesus was—all of them based on almost exactly the same literary documents? Does one have to rely on the opinion of *one* of the so-called "experts" in order to have any opinion of one's own? Was Jesus a magnificent dreamer or a convincing charismatic? Was he an inventor of pithy aphorisms? Was he a revolutionary or a zealous Messianic pretender who tried to force God's hand by offering his life on the cross but failed? We return to the question, Who was Jesus, and whom should I believe?

The answer is not very simple; if it were, it would have been put forward long ago. And part of the reason for the difficulty we face is that what is perceived always involves a perceiver. Nothing is perceived apart from the person who perceives it. If I ask, Who is Jane? the answer will depend on whom I ask. If I ask her husband or partner, I will get one answer. If I ask her daughter, another. If I ask her son, another. A business associate, a friendly neighbor, a jealous competitor, a best friend—each one will perceive Jane differently. So who is Jane? And who is answering "correctly"? Whom should I believe if I have never seen Jane?

Difficulties in Discovering Jesus

Now of course I can get some helpful guidance by finding answers to "historical questions" about her, questions such as, Who were Jane's parents? Where was she born—in what kind of neighborhood? What kind of education did Jane receive? How old is she? Who are her friends? What does she like to do? What is her job? What are her hobbies, or doesn't she have any? And so on and on—the historical questions and their answers are innumerable. A photograph would also help if one were available. And if I were given the opportunity to meet Jane, I would have my own opinion about "who" Jane is, which would be similar in some respects to other opinions I had heard, and completely different in other respects. My opinion would simply add one more to the great number and variety of opinions that exist about who Jane is.

In the case of someone who has died, whom I can never know, I am on far more remote ground than I ever was about Jane, and the disclosure of who the person was becomes much more difficult. In this case the seeker is entirely dependent on stories and documents and traditions originating with the person or with those who knew the person. And so professional historians investigate the known data and, on the basis of their sources, write biographies of people who lived in an earlier time. To become familiar with the subject, the historian must read and reflect. The average person who is not a historian is dependent upon such trained observers to bring to life someone from the past.

When we come to the Gospel narratives about who Jesus was and listen to other early testimonies about Jesus, we are on ground similar to that of every historian of someone who lived in the past. But in Jesus' case we have nothing from the person himself, and nothing from his contemporaries. The earliest Gospel was not written for at least a generation after Jesus' death, and it contains forms of the tradition about Jesus that are from a generation or two later than Jesus, the tradition known in Rome or in some other city of the empire sometime just before or soon after 70 C.E. We do not have a single statement about Jesus that was recorded during Jesus' lifetime. What we have are highly interpreted accounts of what Jesus said or did, written from the perspective of those who were worshipers of Jesus, and the best we can do is try to discover which traditions, in which of their stages of existence, are probably the most "accurate," or "reliable," or "truthful." None of them is "accurate," or "reliable," or "truthful" in the sense in which those words could be used about any living person, or any person only recently deceased.

Let us consider the earliest witness to Jesus on record—that of the apostle Paul. Any reader of Paul's letters will find that what Paul wrote is almost entirely an interpretation of the meaning of Jesus' crucifixion, and very few details arising from Jesus' historical life are revealed. It is for this reason—that Paul's writings are obviously interpretation rather than uninterpreted "fact," as well as because of their position in the canon—that the uninformed reader of the New Testament will assume that the "factual" *Gospels* must have been written before the Pauline interpretation of the significance of the life of Jesus, the person whose "biography" the Gospels narrate. But the historical critic will know that all of Paul's letters were written before any of the Gospels.

Historical criticism tells us that Paul was converted possibly as early as ca. 34 C.E., but not later than 37, and that the earliest letter we have from him is probably 1 Thessalonians, which is usually dated ca. 50–51. That little letter is our earliest witness to Jesus. But Paul's witness is a highly interpreted witness. What Paul "received" about Jesus, and what he subsequently preached, were far from identical. He received the tradition, and then reworked it—it passed through his heart and mind, and became "Pauline." Paul's gospel is, indeed, so stamped by his person that the "Pauline" gospel is fairly easily identified. And this earliest witness to Jesus is still one major step removed from the historical, or real, Jesus.

What is not always realized is that the situation with regard to our earliest Gospel, Mark's Gospel, from a later time than Paul, is not different in principle from what we saw with Paul. Mark also records interpreted tradition about Jesus, which Mark interprets further. Like Paul, Mark was a theologian. Where scholars differ in their interpretation concerning Jesus centers on the selection they make from among the various New Testament—primarily Gospel—traditions, as well as on the way in which they proceed to interpret their selection.

With regard to the interpreter of the Gospels, we encounter the same situation here as in the case of readers and perceivers of any other literature. There are the professional scholars, many of whom have devoted a lifetime to studying the Gospels, or Paul's writings, or other books of the New Testament. Their judgment will carry a certain weight because of their knowledge of the writings and the times from which they come, but each perceiver will also have his or her own perception, and no two perceptions of the literature will be alike.

Every person we know is a person with some significance or other for us, either great or small, either positive, negative, or both. A person devoid of any significance to anyone would be an abstraction. No one knows any such person. We know only the person *together with* the person's significance for somebody. By analogy the same phenomenon prevails in the case of the believer's knowledge of Jesus. Jesus is presented in the church always with a significance that has already been attributed to Jesus. We are enabled to know only a Jesus *together with* a christological overlay, and the New Testament presents us with a great variety of these overlays. Just as we have, for example, Pauline overlays of different varieties, so we also have Marcan overlays, and Matthean overlays, and Lucan overlays, and Johannine overlays. What we must not lose sight of is that Jesus *minus any overlay at all* does not appear in the New Testament and can never be known. Such a Jesus would be someone's abstraction, not a reality.

It is the work of the historical critic to try to come as close as possible to the real person Jesus, the person known by Jesus' contemporaries in Palestine at the beginning of the first century. We have no record of *that* Jesus, written during Jesus' lifetime; we have only later forms of the *tradition* about that Jesus. Whatever picture the historical critic presents us about the actual person Jesus, minus any tradition's witness to that person, can only be a hypothetical abstraction. Already in the earliest Gospel, Mark,

there are christological overlays, and these overlays are sometimes qualified, or added to, by both Matthew and Luke. The fact
that no critic will be able to describe or portray the real Jesus, minus any christological overlay, should in no way discourage the
attempt to get as close as possible to that Jesus, and will not do so;
but the significance for the church of all such portrayals of Jesus
can never be decisive. In the church the lineaments of who Jesus
was will continue to be the figure portrayed in the New Testament. As Luke Johnson has written, "The Gospels . . . provide access to the 'real Jesus' precisely insofar as they reflect the
perception of [Jesus] given by his postresurrection existence."[1]
That is the significance of the canon.

In the church one reads about the historical life of the one believed to be the present, living Sovereign, who is known and believed by the reader to be Savior. The presence of professional
historians in the modern world, who inquire about Jesus as about
every other historical figure, presents the church with the question of the relative weight to be given to the judgments of these
"experts." How definitive are their opinions to be in the church?
Is the judgment of any one of them so significant that it should
displace the judgment of the ordinary Christian reader or
preacher who reads and interprets the Gospels? As Paul Tillich
asked once, Am I to wait for tomorrow's newspaper to learn what
I am to believe? Perhaps a scroll will be discovered that will
negate my entire faith, and I will find out from the *New York
Times* that I, and the whole church, have been wrong all along!
There are many people in the church who are not professional
students of biblical writings but who have spent a lifetime with
the Bible, and their judgments are not to be easily dismissed because they are not professional historians.

Furthermore, the fact remains that the situation with regard to
reading the Gospels is no different from that regarding the study
or "perception" of anyone or anything else. The perceiver and the
perceived always remain in a dialectical relationship, each influ-
encing and being influenced by the other, each questioning and listening to the other. As this dialogue progresses, the perceiver's

Difficulties in Discovering Jesus

understanding is altered; the perceiver shifts ground in relation to the perceived, and at the same time becomes something different.

But we must ask the question, How can we in the church, at the end of the twentieth century, using the Gospels as our primary sources, try to discover who Jesus was—and therefore, who Jesus *is*? What hermeneutical method is available? We shall address this question a little later.

[3]

Gospel Sources and Texts

Sources

We have mentioned the difficult problem of trying to discover precisely which words in the Gospels Jesus actually spoke, and which words probably came from a later time and were ascribed to Jesus by the church. The problem is very complex and results from the fact that what we have in the Gospels are various forms of the tradition that developed over the first two or three generations of the church.

After Jesus' crucifixion-resurrection the tradition about him—what Jesus had said and done—was preserved in the memories of those who had known Jesus, and was handed on orally. The content of what was remembered differed from disciple to disciple, and would be recalled in various discussions and controversies, as well as in connection with preaching and teaching. The question came up, for example, concerning whether believers were to keep the Jewish sabbath. Elsewhere there was the question of whether divorce was to be allowed, and so on—and each time the questions would be answered out of the disciples' memories. This *tradition* (questions and answers) was not written down at first, for a number of reasons: it was not the custom to write down what a teacher had said, even in "schools"; not many people could read; writing materials were scarce and expensive; data about Jesus' words were difficult to collect given the dispersal of the disciples; and, very important, Jesus was expected to return soon—Jesus' "parousia" (literally "presence," or "coming" as the first stage of presence) was anticipated. Paul refers to this parousia often (cf. 1 Thess. 1:9–10).

But later, and gradually, the tradition was preserved in written form, for several reasons: there was the delay in Jesus' coming, the parousia; material was needed for missionary activity; questions emerging in controversies with the Jews had to be answered; words were needed for the instruction and edification of converts; and, finally, there was the biographical motive—who was the Jesus who is preached as the Messiah?

The teaching and preaching of the original disciples was carried out at first only in Palestine, and in the Aramaic dialect. Later the tradition was translated into Greek, probably by bilingual believers. Gentiles spoke Greek, and many Jews inside as well as outside of Palestine spoke Greek—Philo, the great Jewish philosopher in Alexandria, spoke and wrote only in Greek.

Meanwhile Paul, whose language was Greek, was converted, and was traveling and preaching and writing letters—all of them, except for Romans, to his own converts. He had been converted perhaps in 35 C.E. and remained a principal missionary, pastor, and theologian in the church for twenty years or more. He had received the tradition—he had not invented it. It was the tradition about Jesus that had at first so turned him off, but that finally converted him. In 1 Cor. 11:2 Paul writes, "I commend you because . . . you maintain the *traditions* just as I handed them on to you." The word translated "handed on" means, literally, "traditioned." English has the noun "tradition" but not the verb. In Greek, though, there is the verb "to tradition." It is a combination of two words: "to give" and "next to." *To tradition* is to "give next to," to "add to," and "alter." It does not mean *to duplicate unaltered*.

The noun "tradition" in English is often used to speak about repeating what has been done in the past—even sometimes if it was done for the first time only last year. But that is not what the Greek word means. When Paul "traditioned" the "tradition" he did not repeat simply what he had been told. His highly creative mind created a distinctive "Pauline" theology, which was quite different from what we have in the Gospels, or in any other writing. In 1 Cor. 15:3 Paul writes again about "traditioning," which the NRSV translates "handed on." In this case he does apparently repeat what he had been told about Christ's death and resurrection, and Christ's being seen (NRSV "appeared to") by others, but when Paul quotes early formulas they often differ from his own quite unique Pauline theology.

What we have in our four Gospels depends on the source (the origin of the tradition) and on its development up until the point it was used by the evangelist who put it into writing. That is, the content of our Gospels depends on the environment that preserved it.

Mark, like Paul, was an author with a creative mind, who incorporated the *tradition* as it was handed down to him, in the church perhaps in Rome, probably around 68–70. But the tradition Mark received was a living tradition, and continued to develop after Mark had worked with it and written it down. Matthew and Luke also received living tradition. They knew Mark's Gospel and used it in their own respective ways, and passed on in their Gospels the traditions they had received. Matthew and Luke represent the same process of receiving tradition, only at a date later than Mark, and in different locations.

The question of which sayings, parables, and narratives in the Gospels are probably "authentic" (that is, they were actually uttered by Jesus) and which ones entered the tradition later than Jesus as accretions to the earliest tradition, is very complex, and the answers cannot be arrived at by any clear-cut, objective judgment. The Gospels simply do not provide answers to that kind of historical question. The fact that every scholar studying Jesus' life and teaching comes to a conclusion different from that of every other scholar is proof enough that objective data are not available. Everyone who writes a "life of Jesus" produces an image not totally unlike what one sees in a "mirror darkly." The reason is that the contents of the Gospels are not what might be called "factual," but are the written form of oral traditions handed down, over the length of many decades, in various Christian communities. Some of the preserved memories of Jesus undoubtedly correspond closely to early perceptions of what Jesus said or what Jesus did; but other material quite obviously reflects a time in the church that is far later than Jesus. I think we can say with a fair degree of assurance that it is easier to identify late material than it is to be positive about so-called "authentic" material. Later in the chapter we will consider an example of a narrative about a situation in the church that is quite clearly later than Jesus' historical life, the narrative found in Matt. 18:15–35. To illuminate discussion of this text, however, we should review contemporary assumptions that are commonly made with regard to Gospel sources. It is these assumptions that shed light on judgments about the earliest tradition and later developments.

It is now very widely held, although not unanimously, that the Gospels contain either two or four sources, depending on whether one counts two of them as sources. Mark is generally believed to be the oldest Gospel, dating from somewhere around 65–70 C.E. It is also widely believed that about twenty years later Matthew and Luke wrote their Gospels, using Mark as their basic source for the structure of Jesus' life. If one looks at the so-called Synoptic Gospels (Matthew, Mark, and Luke) when laid out in parallel columns,[1] one will see at a glance that those three Gospels have a literary relationship with each other. A "literary relationship" is a way of saying that somebody copied somebody. If, for example, a teacher received three student papers, and each one contained exactly the same sentence or sentences, or approximately the same sentences or paragraphs, the teacher would assume a "literary relationship" between the three papers and would want to have it explained. Without any footnoting one would assume plagiarism: one paper was the original source, and the two other students copied it.

Of course it would be possible to explain the identity of the wording in Matthew, Mark, and Luke by postulating that Jesus often said exactly the same thing three times, and frequently on different occasions and in different contexts, but that explanation would seem a bit farfetched. In the first place, the Synoptic Gospels contain *stories about* Jesus—not only Jesus' sayings—described in the same words. Also the introductions to Jesus' words are often found verbatim, or nearly so. And the narratives about Jesus are more often than not in the same order.

Even more unlikely would be the assumption that not only did Jesus say the same thing in Aramaic at three different times, but that every time Jesus said the same thing in Aramaic, it was translated into exactly the same Greek. It is the Greek form of Jesus' sayings that is identical, the Gospels having been written in Greek. The assumption of a literary relationship, of a copying of the same Greek words by different writers, best explains the verbatim relationship of the Gospels—that Matthew and Luke depended on and copied the Greek words of Mark.

There are many examples of parallels between Matthew, Mark, and Luke such as Matt. 3:13–17, Mark 1:9–11, and Luke 3:21–22. This is narrative material. The words are not Jesus' words (only the last words are a quotation), but they are nevertheless nearly verbatim, even though it would not seem to be important to quote them exactly. It is also interesting to note that in quoting the words spoken by the Holy Spirit, Matthew does not copy Mark exactly. Whereas Mark represents the Spirit as saying to Jesus, "You are my Son, the Beloved; with you I am well pleased" (Mark 1:11), Matthew has "*This is* my Son, the Beloved, with *whom* I am well pleased" (Matt. 3:17). In Mark the voice from heaven addresses Jesus, but Matthew has the voice announce to those in proximity— John the Baptist and "many Pharisees and Sadducees" (Matt. 3:7)— that "This one [not 'You'] is my Son, with whom [rather than 'with you'] I am well pleased." One notes that Matthew feels free here to alter words represented by Mark as spoken by the Holy Spirit; Matthew also, throughout his Gospel, frequently changes words that Mark tells us were spoken by *Jesus.* The tradition, which included Jesus' words, was still in flux, and the words of the tradition were considered alterable by those who received them. It was not until a much later time that the church was to hold that words of the tradition were not to be changed; but the church did not canonize *words,* it canonized *books.* Not only Matthew's and Luke's use of Mark, but textual criticism in general, make it evident that the words of the Gospels were not considered sacred and unchangeable.

Let us look at another Synoptic parallel, this one involving a dialogue that includes Jesus: Matt. 12:1–8, Mark 2:23–28, and Luke

6:1–5. The passage, found in all three Gospels, is a dialogue between Jesus and Pharisees. The words are very similar in all three Gospels, with Matthew and Luke occasionally abbreviating Mark. We should remember that the Gospel authors wrote on rolls, probably made of papyri, and these rolls, unlike codices or books, would break if they were longer than roughly the length of our Gospel of Matthew. So authors had to calculate carefully in advance the length of the various materials they intended to include. Matthew and Luke had other sources besides Mark that they wanted to copy, so they eliminated some of Mark's words in the interest of saving space.

We note, for example, that they both omitted "and as they made their way" from Mark 2:23, which it was not necessary to add after saying that Jesus "was going through the grainfields." Matthew and Luke also did not need to add Mark's "and in need of food" to the words "when they were hungry" (Mark 2:25). Another very interesting omission from both Matthew and Luke is Mark's "when Abiathar was high priest" (Mark 2:26). The probable reason for this omission was that Mark had made a mistake. According to 1 Sam. 21:1–6, the high priest at the time of the incident involving David was Ahimelech, not Abiathar. Matthew and Luke may very well have noted the error and skipped it.

Interesting, also, is the omission by both Matthew and Luke of Mark's words, spoken by Jesus: "The sabbath was made for the human being, and not the human being for the sabbath" (Mark 2:27, author's translation). Though Mark quotes the words as spoken by Jesus, both Matthew and Luke eliminate them. Once again, the tradition, even of words spoken by Jesus, was thought of as fluid and not frozen, and whole statements of Jesus could be omitted apparently without any feelings of guilt.

It will be seen that in Matt. 12:5–7 the evangelist has added what he represents as a quotation of Jesus, which he did not get from Mark. He has Jesus say first, in v. 5, that according to the law there is precedent for doing work on the sabbath: "the priests in the temple break the sabbath and yet are guiltless." And indeed, according to Num. 28:9–10, the daily burnt offering was to be doubled on the sabbath, and according to Lev. 24:8 it was on the sabbath that the priests set out the bread of the presence in the temple. It was by referring to the work that the priests did on the sabbath that Matthew placed the activity of Jesus' disciples in the context of the law. The Pharisees should have no objection to what the disciples did, for there were precedents in the activity of the priests—precedents cited in Hebrew scripture.

Matthew then has Jesus add, "I tell you, something greater than the temple is here" (Matt. 12:6). Matthew is arguing from the lesser to the greater: If the law allowed work to be done on the sabbath by the priests in the temple, how much more permissible it is that work be allowed on the sabbath in the case of the disciples of the Messiah! Something much greater than the temple was present—either Jesus himself, or perhaps the community around Jesus. Then Matthew has Jesus quote Hos. 6:6, "I desire mercy and not sacrifice." The Pharisees should have had mercy on Jesus' hungry disciples, rather than blaming them for doing what the Pharisees mistakenly thought was forbidden by the law. And finally, Jesus tells the Pharisees that if they had understood Hosea they would not have "condemned the guiltless." The disciples were "guiltless" because they were protected by the Messiah. So the words of v. 8, taken from Mark, "The Son of Man is lord of the sabbath," following as it does Matthew's insertion of vv. 5–7, have a greatly increased christological significance.

The "Q" Source

In addition to using Mark, most critics also postulate that Matthew and Luke had in common a second source, which is referred to as "Q" from the first letter of the German word for "source," which is *Quelle*. It was thought that the letter "Q" would not beg any questions about the age or character of the source. It would be a neutral term. This source does not exist separately from its use in the Gospels, but it is postulated because of the many verbal agreements between Matthew and Luke that are not taken from Mark. Since we *have* Mark and know that many verbal agreements between Matthew and Luke did not come from Mark, we must postulate that they were taken from a second source.

Gospel Sources and Texts

.   As an example of the use of Q by Matthew and Luke, look at
the following parallel: Matt. 12:41–42 = Luke 11:31–32. Except
for two very small differences, the wording of Matthew and Luke
is exactly the same. Matthew does not have Luke's "the people of "
(Matt. 12:42), which requires that Matthew write "and condemn
it," while Luke has "and condemn *them*" (Luke 11:31). Otherwise,
Matthew and Luke are in perfect agreement. One must therefore
postulate that lying behind Matthew and Luke is a source they
shared in common. The only alternative to that would be to suppose that either Matthew or Luke copied the other one. This alternative is occasionally held, but most scholars reject it because it
creates some enormous problems of its own.

So the two-document hypothesis is that Mark and Q were the
sources used by Matthew and Luke. There is, however, a good deal
of material that is unique to Matthew and unique to Luke. In fact,
some of the best known parables and stories of the Gospels are
found only in one or the other Gospel. The story of the visit of the
Magi to Bethlehem at Jesus' birth (Matt. 2:1–12); the parables
of the ten bridesmaids (25:1–13), the laborers in the vineyard
(20:1–16), the unmerciful servant (18:23–35), and the two sons
(21:28–32) — are all found only in Matthew; and in Luke only we
have the story of the appearance of the angels to shepherds at the
time of Jesus' birth (2:1–20); and the parables of the good Samar-
itan (10:29–37), the prodigal son (15:11–32), the Pharisee and
the publican (18:9–14), and the rich fool (12:13–21). Only in
Matthew's birth narrative do we have the story of the flight into
Egypt and Herod's killing of the babies (2:13–16); only in Luke's
birth narrative do we have the Magnificat (1:46–56). Where did all
these parables and stories come from? What was their source?
Some scholars believe that both Matthew and Luke had independent written sources that are imaginatively designated "M" for
Matthew and "L" for Luke. With those two additional sources one
would postulate four sources for the Gospels. But other scholars
are not willing to describe the special material in Matthew and
Luke as sources, or at least as written sources, and prefer to speak
only of *two* written sources, Mark and Q.

Jesus Christ

An Example of a Narrative
Arising Later than Jesus' Time

Unless one reads the Gospels assuming that every word attributed to Jesus was spoken by him just as the text says, one would probably conclude that the narrative and discussion of Matt. 18:15–35 reflects a situation in the church near the end of the first century, later than Jesus' time, that was familiar to the writer of Matthew. In the first place, the narrative concerns the relationship to the "church" of one who has sinned (see Matt. 18:17). The word "church" is primarily a Pauline word in the New Testament, appearing in only two places in all four Gospels, both of them in Matthew. The first occurrence is in Matt. 16:18, where Jesus says to Peter, "You are Peter, and on this rock I will build my church"; the second is in Matt. 18:17. In Matt. 18:15 Jesus is represented as saying to "the disciples" (18:1), "If your brother (NRSV "another member of the church") sins against you, go and point out the fault when the two of you are alone"; and in 18:17 Jesus says, "If he (i.e., the "brother" or "member") refuses to listen to them, tell it to the church; and if (the offender) refuses to listen to the church, let such a one be to you as a Gentile and a tax collector" (v. 17). These are the only places in the Gospels where the word "church" occurs.

The reference to the "church" in Matt. 16:18 and 18:17 assumes, of course, the formation and the existence of "church" at the time these words were written. In 18:15–17 the author of Matthew represents the threefold practice of the Matthean community by which a member of the community who has sinned is to be restored to the community. But perhaps Matthew's point in these three verses is oriented even more to the necessity of excluding the sinner when all exhortations to repent have failed. (In the rough parallel in Luke 17:3 the point is more clearly that the sinner should be forgiven.) The threefold rule laid out in Matthew is as follows: (1) The person who has been offended is to point out the offense to the offender; (2) if the offender does not "listen" to the one offended, one or two other people are to be brought along to confirm what is said; and (3) if the offender does not listen even to them, the matter is to be brought before the "church," that is, the congregation, and the person will become "as a Gentile and a tax collector." Clearly reflected here is a development in the life of a local congregation that came into being long after the time of the historical life of Jesus.

We must note, however, that the rule for reconciling a sinner to the church community, or for putting out a sinner who would not own up to sinning—a rule that developed in the life of the Matthean congregation—is represented by Matthew as having been handed down by Jesus. The disciples ask "Jesus" a question in Matt. 18:1, and Jesus' answer begins in v. 3 and extends through v. 20. Then in v. 21 Peter asks Jesus another question, and this time Jesus' answer begins in v. 22 and moves on to include the parable of the unmerciful servant in vv. 23–35. These words, though spoken by the Sovereign in the church, were not spoken by the historical Jesus, but were nevertheless heard in the church as Jesus' words. The church did not understand that words spoken by Jesus to the *church* were any less authoritative than words spoken by the historical person Jesus to the *disciples*. Both "words" were heard as words of Jesus. It is for this reason that the modern critical student of the Bible sometimes has great difficulty in separating early and later words of Jesus between which the early church made no distinction. The question of which words of Jesus were spoken by the historical person while he was here on earth is a modern question. It was not a question in which the Gospel authors had any interest, and they give us no clues as to how to answer it. The critic must work only with guesses and hypotheses.

We should also note that the *tradition* in the church took different forms in different places and at different times. Various churches had their own forms of the tradition. Not even the prayer Jesus taught his disciples to pray was handed down and said in the same form in different places. The church says the form of the prayer as it appears in Matt. 6:9–13. Luke's form of the prayer, found in Luke 11:2–4, has the same canonical authority as Matthew's but is not a part of the church's liturgical life, and many Christians do not even know that the Gospels record Jesus' prayer in two different forms. There is also a third form of the prayer, found in the second-century document known as the *Didache*. Which of the several prayers represented in the New Testament and the *Didache* did Jesus teach the disciples to pray? Or does none of them represent Jesus' word? It is an interesting fact that that question has not been a concern of the church, which since very early times has said the "Lord's Prayer" as it appears in Matthew, without ever asking the modern question of "authenticity" with regard to it. Matthew tells us that Jesus taught the prayer Matthew records, and the fact that the accuracy of Matthew's record here is highly questionable today in no way has affected the church's practice of using it as the prayer Jesus taught us to pray. This says something significant and provocative about the weight (or lack of it) carried by the observations and dicta of historical critics in the daily life of the church.

Another question: What did Jesus say at the Last Supper? Surely the church has remembered those words exactly, regardless of what source one goes to! But in fact, in the three Gospels we have three different accounts of what Jesus said. Over the bread Matthew reports Jesus as saying, "Take, eat; this is my body" (26:26); but Mark leaves out "eat" in the sentence (14:22), and Luke has Jesus saying much more than either Matthew or Mark. In Luke Jesus says, "This is my body," (omitting both verbs, "take" and "eat"), adding, "which is given for you. Do this in remembrance of me" (22:19).

Likewise over the cup Jesus' words are different in all three Gospels. The differences in the words Jesus speaks in the Gospels reflect differences in the liturgies of the churches from which the Gospels came; but once again, the interesting fact is that insofar as the church's worship is concerned, any one of them is as usable as any other one, and no one asks which words are "authentic," refusing to participate in the Supper because of the historical-critical answer to that question.

And if one asks about what Jesus said from the cross, once again we have three different accounts. Matthew (27:46) and Mark (15:34) report Jesus as saying, "My God, my God, why have you forsaken me?" which Jesus says in either Aramaic (Mark) or Hebrew (Matthew). They are the only words Jesus speaks from the cross in those Gospels. But Luke does not have Jesus saying either of those words. In Luke Jesus makes two quite different statements. The first one, which is omitted in some very old and reliable manuscripts, is a prayer: "Father, forgive them; for they do not know what they are doing." It is Jesus' prayer for the two criminals crucified on either side of him (23:34). The second statement in Luke is made directly to one of the criminals, "Truly I tell you, today you will be with me in Paradise" (23:43).

In the Gospel of John Jesus speaks three times from the cross. The first time he addresses his mother and the disciple whom he loved, both of whom were standing near the cross. To his mother Jesus says, "Woman, here is your son," and to the disciple he says, "Here is your mother." After this Jesus says, "I am thirsty," and finally Jesus says, "It is finished." Once again, the tradition about what Jesus said differed from place to place, taking different forms as it developed.

Texts or Manuscripts

There is another matter, aside from the matter of sources, which occasionally has a bearing on the question of exactly which words in our Gospels were spoken by Jesus, and that is the matter of *texts* or *manuscripts*. Many readers of the Gospels—or, for that matter, many readers of the Bible—are not aware that the translation they are reading represents a selection of texts that were chosen by the translators as *probably* what was originally written. Not a single *autograph* of a biblical writing—that is, no writing as it came from its author—has survived. What we have are *copies* of writings, and most of them very *late* copies. Our earliest sources for what was written are only small fragments of copies.

The earliest extant fragment of a New Testament writing is a small piece of papyrus containing a few words of the Gospel of John, from about 125–150 C.E., and there are ten other Christian biblical manuscripts from the second century, all of them papyrus. The earliest copies of the whole New Testament date from around

350–400 C.E., and these are written on vellum (tanned animal skin). Today there are in the world more than 5000 manuscripts, and fragments of manuscripts of parts or the whole of the New Testament, the earliest of which were not known until they were found in the last century. What do these many manuscripts reveal?

In the first place, they have all been cataloged, and their readings have been noted. Any Greek New Testament represents what its editor or editors believe were probably the words that were originally written. The same is true of an English translation—it translates the Greek text believed by the translator or translators to represent the most likely original one, drawn from and created out of all the extant manuscripts. No English New Testament corresponds exactly to any Greek manuscript. How does one learn what are the readings of the thousands of extant manuscripts?

Of course no one person can discover for himself or herself what is written in every manuscript. But as noted above, manuscripts have been classified and cataloged according to their particular readings, and if a Greek New Testament has an *apparatus* in the footnotes, it will disclose various important readings that are known. Usually only two or perhaps three major so-called "variants" are given; occasionally there are more.

Why are there variant readings? Why aren't all manuscripts of biblical books the same? One reason is that it is impossible to copy perfectly by hand. Even with electric lights and eyeglasses, copyists still make mistakes. And even those who proofread what has been written often miss some typographical errors. Copyists get tired copying hour after hour, and sometimes they skip whole lines—their eyes go back to the wrong place on what they are copying, and sometimes they copy the same words more than once.

But many times a copyist of the Gospels will have deliberately made one Gospel conform to another—almost always Mark or Luke harmonized with Matthew. For example, Luke wrote that Jesus continued to proclaim the message "in the synagogues of Judea" (4:44). But Matthew and Mark both said, in parallel passages, that Jesus was proclaiming "throughout *Galilee*" (Matt. 4:23; Mark 1:39). So a scribe copying Luke, who knew that in other Gospels Jesus was said to have taught in Galilee, altered Luke 4:44 to read that Jesus proclaimed the message "in the synagogues of Galilee." That is the reading of many Greek manuscripts of Luke. It is those late manuscripts that were used by the translators of the King James Version, so if one reads the King James of Luke 4:44 one will read: "And he preached in the synagogues of Galilee." The King James Version was based on late manuscripts. Much earlier, more correct manuscripts were not known then.

But that is not the end of the story. Another scribe came along in the fifth century who knew that some manuscripts of Luke read "Judea" and others read "Galilee"; so not knowing which was correct, the scribe wrote that Jesus proclaimed the message "in the synagogues of the Jews." That would cover either "Galilee" or "Judea," and the scribe would not be making a mistake!

A good example of a discrepancy in the Gospels about exactly what Jesus said may be found in comparing Matt. 7:9–10 with Luke 11:11–12. Here we find a copyist who appears to have harmonized Luke with Matthew. Luke probably wrote: "Is there anyone among you who, if your child asks for a fish, will give a snake instead of a fish? Or if the child asks for an egg, will give a scorpion?" That is the text translated in the NRSV and in most recent translations. But Matthew's parallel is different. Matthew has: "Is there anyone among you who, *if your child asks for bread, will give a stone*? Or if the child asks for a fish, will give a snake?" A scribe who knew Matthew noticed that one of Matthew's examples of what one would not do was missing in Luke, so he added Matthew's "if your child asks for bread, will give a stone," and has Jesus give three examples of inhuman acts, rather than two. Did Jesus give two examples? And if so, were they the ones quoted in Matthew, or in Luke? Or does the longer reading in Luke quote Jesus accurately? The King James Version has the longer reading because the translators did not know the earlier manuscripts that have been found in the last century and a half. Which words Jesus actually said is a textual matter, having nothing to do with translation. Differences in English translations of the Bible often reflect differences in manuscripts as well as differences in translation of the same words.

Another interesting *textual* matter is to be found in Matt. 27:16–17, where, once again, we find differences in various English translations. Until recently, translations always read something like this: (v. 16) "And they had a notorious prisoner called Barabbas. (v. 17) So when they had gathered, Pilate said to them, 'Whom do you want me to release for you, Barabbas or Jesus who is called Christ?'" (RSV). But if one reads more recent translations one comes upon a very different question asked by Pilate. The NRSV reads: (v. 16) "At that time they had a notorious prisoner, called Jesus Barabbas. (v. 17) So after they had gathered, Pilate said to them, 'Whom do you want me to release for you, Jesus Barabbas or Jesus who is called the Messiah?'"

The difference between "the Messiah" in the NRSV and "Christ" in the RSV is a difference in *translation* of the *same* Greek word; but the difference between "Jesus Barabbas" and "Barabbas" in vv. 16 and 17 is a *textual* difference. Most manuscripts of Matthew have simply "Barabbas," but a few manuscripts identify the "notorious prisoner" as "*Jesus* Barabbas." These manuscripts, though few in number, undoubtedly represent Matthew's original text. Pilate's question then becomes, Which *Jesus* do you want me to release—Jesus who is Barabbas, or Jesus who is called the Messiah? The name "Jesus" as referring to Barabbas was probably dropped out of Matthew's original text in reverence for the name, which, it was thought, could not have been the name of a sinner. In fact, in most languages spoken today "Jesus" is still not used as a proper name—the most notable exception, of course, being Spanish.

With regard to the prayer Jesus taught the disciples to pray, the church uses the form of the prayer preserved in Matt. 6:9–13, but the *text* of that prayer, also, differs in various manuscripts. The oldest manuscripts do not contain the doxology at the end of the prayer, and neither does the translation called the Vulgate; hence the Roman Catholic Church does not say it. Furthermore, the doxology is written in three different ways in the manuscripts, the form used by the church having by all odds the strongest and best support.

Gospel Sources and Texts

It is clear that the tradition differs considerably in different places and at different times. Not even the prayer Jesus taught the disciples to pray was preserved in the same form in the Gospels. The desire to know exactly what Jesus said, and under what circumstances, cannot be fulfilled. The ancient Gospels, which are our primary sources for such information, do not answer our modern questions. But we can note that the life and faith of Christian believers, and the questions and answers of New Testament scholars, seem to go along in parallel with each other, seldom intersecting. While this is most unfortunate, it is also understandable because of too great claims made by the critics. The results of the investigations of New Testament scholars are relevant to the church's faith, but they cannot presume to govern it. They play an important role, but it is never overriding. Biblical scholarship is properly a tool of the church, not the church's master, and if biblical critics are not first and foremost believers, Jewish or Christian, their witness is suspect and of marginal significance to the believing congregation. If the scholar works within the context of the believing community, and if the work of the scholar is at the same time the work of the believer, the church and the scholar are working not against each other, but toward a common end.

[4]

The Dominion
of God

In spite of the impossibility of our knowing precisely what Jesus said and did—and when, and where, and why, and under what circumstances, it is not sensible or logical also to assume that the Gospels give us no information about who Jesus was, and what Jesus said and did. It would be unreasonable to believe that almost all the earliest narratives about Jesus are fabrications, that almost all authentic memories of Jesus disappeared after two generations, and that what the church preserved about Jesus is largely invention. Certainly the church does not believe, and has never believed, that the identity of the Sovereign and Savior it worships, who reveals who God is, is unknowable, and therefore is only what the church has concocted. The church has always believed, and continues to believe, that the Jesus who speaks and acts in the Gospels was a concrete human being—"Christ Jesus, who, though being in the form of God, did not regard equality with God as something to be exploited, but emptied Christ's self, taking the form of a servant, (and was) born in human likeness," and "became flesh" (cf. Phil. 2:6–7 [Inclusive Version] and John 1:14). And the belief remains in the worshiping community that it has preserved tradition about that Sovereign and Savior in its Gospels particularly, but also elsewhere throughout the New Testament. The church cannot be convinced that the person, Jesus, who became worshiped in the church as the second Person of the Trinity, was so innocuous in reality that later disciples had to formulate his identity. Of course not every detail of what all four Gospels tell us that Jesus said or did can be accepted as precise remembrance of Jesus from some particular point of view—obviously the Gospels do not agree among themselves on the subject. But that does not mean that the testimony in general one finds in the Gospels is off-center and irrelevant.

When one inquires, however, about *specific* content of Jesus' teaching and preaching, the answer becomes, as we have seen, somewhat problematic. It has become quite difficult for anyone to state that Jesus said or taught or did such and such things, without any doubt whatsoever. Regarding details, one can only rely on one's best judgment, having investigated the matter the best one can. A number of New Testament scholars who have studied the Gospels critically have held that Jesus was an eschatological preacher of the "dominion of God."[1] The term is used 149 times in the New Testament, and of those, 118 occur in the Synoptic Gospels. The term is basically a Synoptic Gospel term, occurring only thirty-one times in the remainder of the New Testament—five times in the Gospel of John, and twenty-six times elsewhere. It is in the Synoptic Gospels primarily that the historical person Jesus is closely associated with the preaching of the dominion of God, a term that otherwise was seldom used in the earliest literature of the church. Some of the more radical recent critics have tended to discount Jesus as a preacher of the dominion of God, and have argued for a number of different ways to identify Jesus.

It seems, not only to me, but to many other scholars as well, that the evidence for the eschatological Jesus remains very strong; and the evidence for Jesus as a preacher of *the dominion of God* is too significant to be displaced by arguments to the contrary. So I will now try to illuminate the testimony of the Gospels regarding what I consider to be the major thrust of Jesus' preaching.

With the exception of the Gospel of Matthew, the expression used in the New Testament is always "dominion of *God.*" In Matthew the term is usually "dominion of *heaven,*" which Matthew uses 32 times. Five times in Matthew's Gospel the expression is "dominion of *God.*" It has been pretty well demonstrated that there is no difference in the meaning of the two terms. Matthew preferred not to refer directly to God, but to use the Jewish circumlocution "heaven" for "God." In two other instances Matthew also avoids referring to "God" by means of the circumlocution "Father," speaking of "the dominion of their (or my) Father," rather than of "God" (Matt. 13:43; 26:29). Mark's parallel to Matt. 26:29 is "dominion of *God.*" Matt. 13:43 has no parallel in either of the other Gospels.

With regard to the meaning of the term "dominion of God," there is wide agreement that in *Jewish* literature, when the word "dominion" is applied to God, it always means "monarchical rule" and not "place" or "kingdom." It describes the sovereignty or rule of the monarch, not the territory over which the monarch rules. Psalm 145:11–13 illustrates this Jewish meaning very clearly, where "power," "mighty deeds," and "rule" are used as synonyms for "dominion"—all the terms referring to the exertion of authority, and none of them to the place over which authority is exercised.

> They shall speak of the glory of your *dominion,*
> and tell of your *power,*
> to make known to all people your *mighty acts,*
> and the glorious splendor of your *dominion.*
> Your *dominion* is everlasting,
> and your *rule* endures throughout all generations.
>
> (Ps. 145:11–13,
author's translation)

Let us discuss now the English words "kingdom" and "dominion." The usual English translation of the New Testament Greek word is "kingdom" of God. Why, then, translate it "dominion"? The reason is that the Greek word has two connotations. It connotes both the *exercise of authority* and the *place where authority is exercised.* Or, to put it another way, it means *rule* or *reign* as well as *realm* or *kingdom.* The English word "kingdom" covers only one of the possible meanings of the Greek word, and does not connote the exercise of authority.

It must be said that in much preaching and teaching in the church the word "kingdom" is interpreted as though it meant "rule": the "kingdom" of God is treated as though it meant the

The Dominion of God

"rule" of God. "Kingdom of God" is also widely interpreted, however, to mean "realm" of God, interpreters using both words, "rule" and "realm," for "kingdom." Strictly speaking, the English word "realm" is a near synonym for "kingdom," but "rule" is not. A kingdom is a *place* ruled by a king, and a realm is also a *place* over which there is a ruler; but in ordinary English usage a kingdom does not *rule,* does not exert authority, but is the *place* where authority is exercised.

The word "dominion," unlike "kingdom," means both rule and realm. One may enter into a dominion, as one may enter into a kingdom; but while one also exercises *dominion over,* one cannot exercise *kingdom over.* So the English word "dominion" is a more adequate translation of the Greek word than "kingdom" is because "dominion," like the Greek word it translates, has two meanings. The translation "dominion" has another advantage over "kingdom"—it is not as blatantly androcentric, or "male-centered." The word "kingdom" keeps reminding one of the authority of a male ruler, a king, who is in charge, in a way scarcely approximated by the word "dominion."

Unless the Synoptic Gospels are far off the mark in their frequent representations of Jesus as a preacher of the dominion of God, it would appear that the "dominion of God" was the focus of his preaching. At the beginning of his Gospel, Mark says that after Jesus was baptized and had received the Spirit, and after John was arrested, Jesus went into Galilee preaching the gospel of God and saying, "The time is fulfilled, and *the dominion of God* has come near; repent, and believe in the gospel" (Mark 1:15). Throughout the Gospels the theme of that specific preaching of Jesus recurs, and it is very hard to interpret the Gospels if one has no notion of what Jesus meant by "dominion of God." So let us try to understand what was in Jesus' mind when he used the term, and what the disciples understood when they heard Jesus use it. How is one to understand the term today, and how is one to preach it?

Almost everyone who has written about Jesus' preaching has discussed this question, and one can read histories of the interpretation of "dominion of God." This book is an attempt not to review what has been written in the past, but to elucidate, from one point of view, one aspect of what Jesus was referring to by "dominion of God."

Any study of the Gospels, any critical study of any part of the Bible, must bring historical criticism to bear on the text, just as in the attempt to increase an understanding of any literature, one must use historical-critical tools. The use of the tools is not an end in itself; it contributes to the understanding of the text. In the case of the term "dominion of God," historical criticism raises the question of Jesus' intention in using the term, and of what the original hearers of the term understood by it. Another, separate question revolves around the issue of what each of the biblical authors who use the term meant by it. What Jesus meant by the term, and what the author of the Gospel of Matthew, for example, interpreted the term to mean, are two different questions having two different sets of answers.

But historical criticism is a modern method of inquiry. It did not exist in its present form until the eighteenth century, when Reimarus asserted, for example, that faith and reason are irreconcilable and that the disciples deliberately misled others about who Jesus was. But critical discussion of the meaning of the specific term "dominion of God" did not arise until early in the nineteenth century, when Friedrich Schleiermacher published his great work, *The Christian Faith*.[2] Schleiermacher interpreted the life of Jesus in accordance with rationalistic principles. He had no interest in the historical question of who Jesus was and what Jesus might have meant by the term "dominion of God"; he simply adopted Jesus' term for his own theological purposes, as though it were his own. For Schleiermacher, the dominion of God was the corporate life together of Christians in communion with God, made possible by Christ.

Schleiermacher, who dominated the Protestant German thought of his time, was followed by Albrecht Ritschl, who was a historian and an exegete, but became most widely known as a theologian. Ritschl was interested in trying to find the essence of

The Dominion of God

Christianity, as opposed to what he called its "accidents." The center of his theology became humanity and its spiritual needs. One of Ritschl's emphases was that Christianity offered freedom from individual guilt, made possible by Christ. His other major emphasis was the concept of the dominion of God: Christians, reconciled with one another and working in harmony together out of the impulse of love, under the "Fatherhood" of God, were to build the ideal community or society, which Ritschl identified as the dominion of God.

The nineteenth century also produced numerous attempts at writing a "life of Jesus." By far the most popular of them was Ernest Renan's *The Life of Jesus*.[3] Published in June of 1863, it had already run to ten editions by the end of the year, and by 1923 there had been 205 editions in French and 216 in other languages. It appears safe to say that no other life of Jesus ever reached so wide a public. But its critical worth is not very great, in spite of the fact that Renan wrote in his preface: "I have written my book with the cold candour of a historian, with the single aim of discovering the finest and most exact shades of truth."[4] Renan, like many since him, was confident that he had unveiled for the world a picture of Jesus that corresponded to the truth, yet a twentieth-century historian wrote of Renan's portrait: "Jesus is presented as a kind of gentle dreamer who wanders through the countryside of Galilee smiling at life."[5] That characterization of Renan's "Life" sounds very much like the liberal sentimentality of the eighteenth century. Renan conceived the dominion of God as the inheritance primarily of children and the poor. He wrote that for Jesus, "The Gospel . . . is made for the poor; it is to them he brings the glad tidings of salvation."[6]

Renan concluded that Jesus had been a pious peasant who went out among the poor and the disinherited. Nineteenth-century lives of Jesus repeatedly represented nineteenth-century views of what the ideal person would be like. Jesus was read in terms of the times. But for one nineteenth-century critic, Bruno Bauer, Jesus never existed at all.[7] Historical criticism may truly lead anywhere!

Jesus Christ

The Emergence of Hermeneutics

At the very end of the last century a historical critic of the New Testament produced a "life of Jesus" that turned out to be a bombshell. His name was Johannes Weiss, and he was extremely critical of the blatant way in which so-called historians had been interpreting the life of first-century Jesus as though he were one of their contemporaries, with typical nineteenth-century beliefs about the characteristics of a noble human being. Such "lives of Jesus," Weiss believed, could hardly claim to be "historical."

In 1892 Weiss, professor of New Testament at Marburg University, published *The Preaching of Jesus on the Kingdom of God*,[8] a little book of sixty-seven pages, in which he expressed some satisfaction in the fact that theologians were dealing with the important subject of "dominion of God," but he greatly regretted that they had shown no interest in the fundamental question of what in the world Jesus had meant by the term. Where was their historical sense? Theologians were using the term "dominion of God" as if they had invented it, as if it were not rooted in Jesus' first-century preaching in Palestine. Weiss warned that historical inquiry demanded that the term be interpreted in first-century Jewish terms that were consistent also with Jesus' views as expressed elsewhere in the Gospels. The expression "dominion of God" was not a cipher into which anyone could pour whatever ideas were dear to one's heart.

Weiss's position might seem obvious, but it turned out not to be obvious at all, and, in fact, it does not appear yet to have caught on everywhere. His radical interpretation of "dominion of God" created such a storm of protest that he produced a second edition of his book, now expanded to 214 pages. In these works Weiss developed three major criticisms of Ritschl.[9]

First of all, Weiss said, in using the term "dominion of God" Ritschl and others did not do justice to the antithesis between the dominion of *God* and the dominion of *Satan* in Jesus' preaching, an antithesis that is often found in Jewish apocalyptic literature. For example, in chapter 10 of the Jewish *Assumption of Moses* (its date is uncertain, but it may come from the time of Jesus), we find the following:

And then shall [God's] kingdom appear throughout all [God's]
creation;
And then shall the Devil meet the Devil's end,
And sorrow shall depart with the Devil. . . .
For the Heavenly One will [arise] from the royal throne,
And go forth from the holy dwelling-place
With wrath and anger because of the offspring of the
Heavenly One.
And the earth will tremble:
It will be shaken to its farthest bounds;
And high mountains will collapse
And hills will be shaken and fall.
And the sun will not give *its* light;
And the horns of the moon will be turned into darkness,
And they will be broken,
And the moon will be turned wholly into blood. . . .
For the Most High will arise, the Eternal God alone,
And [God] will appear to punish the Gentiles,
And . . . will destroy all their idols.
Then happy will you be, Israel;
And you will trample upon the necks of the Gentiles . . .
And God will exalt you . . .
And you will look from on high and see your enemies on earth,
And you will recognize them and rejoice,
And give thanks and confess your Creator.

$$(10:1-10).^{10}$$

To the words of this first-century Jewish writing compare Jesus'
words in Matt. 12:25–29: "If Satan casts out Satan, Satan is divided; how then will Satan's dominion stand?" But Satan was not
"divided," and did not self-destruct. Satan was powerful and had
"possessed" a person who was blind and mute. It took the power
of Jesus to overcome Satan. Weiss maintained that any discussion
of "dominion of God" must reflect that great enmity between Jesus
and the power of evil, an enmity between God and Satan that is
clearly delineated also in Jewish apocalyptic literature.

Second, said Weiss, Ritschl emphasized the activity of human beings in "building" God's dominion, whereas Jesus emphasized the activity of God as Monarch. God's dominion, for Jesus, is not *built* or *furthered* by human endeavor; it is established only by God: Jesus preached the coming of the dominion of *God,* not of even the most beneficent human being. The dominion of God is the final incursion of God into history, having the same character as the onslaught of the Flood in primordial times. Note Jesus' analogy: "Just as it was in the days of Noah, so too it will be in the days of the Human One. They were eating and drinking, and marrying and being given in marriage, until the day Noah entered the ark, and the flood came and destroyed all of them" (Luke 17:26–27 = Matt. 24:37–39a, Inclusive Version). In the same way, by the same monarchical power, God will establish God's "dominion."

Finally, Weiss said that Ritschl saw the intention of Jesus as being to inaugurate a development in the first century that would finally, after many centuries, issue in the moral reorganization of humanity. Human hard work and moral rectitude would at last bring to fulfillment what Jesus had begun. But, said Weiss, Jesus did not believe he was beginning a movement that would be carried on into the nineteenth century. Jesus believed, rather, that he was standing at the *end* of history. The one thing yet to be accomplished was the judgment of God, which would be followed by the consummation of all things, the dominion of God—none of it in human hands at all.

Weiss insisted that Jesus should be understood against the background of prophetic and apocalyptic Judaism. And the prophets and apocalyptists spoke of God as the overruling Monarch who would bring about a great natural and historical crisis. Isaiah 40:10 says:

> Behold, the Sovereign God comes with *power*
> (Cf. Mark 1:7: "The one *more powerful* than I comes after me"),
>> And God's arm *rules* for God;
>> behold, God's reward is with God,
>>> and God's recompense before God.
>
> (author's translation)

Note also Zechariah 14:9:

The Dominion of God

> And God will become monarch over all the earth; on
> that day God will be one, and God's name one.
>
> (author's translation)

These prophets and seers all looked forward in hope to the day when God as Monarch would redeem God's people, when God would take up God's great power and put down all Israel's enemies, and finally crush the evil that is now rampant everywhere. Weiss believed that Jesus expected this final, cataclysmic, victorious event to occur in the near future. The same occurrence that Jesus' predecessors had looked forward to in hope, Jesus expected would take place immediately. God, the Sovereign and Monarch of the world, was about to exert God's final power and rule.

According to Jesus, then, said Weiss, establishment of the dominion of God would have nothing to do with any social or political activity of men and women, but was entirely in the hands of God. There would be no "evolving" of the dominion, no human constructing of it. Rather Jesus taught the disciples to pray, "May your dominion *come*" (Matt. 6:10, author's translation)—not evolve, or develop. Weiss also quoted Jesus' words: "It is God's good pleasure to *give* you the dominion" (Luke 12:32, Inclusive Version), and, "If it is by the Spirit of God that I cast out demons, then the dominion of God *has come* to you" (Matt. 12:28 = Luke 11:20). These quotations from Jesus (and Weiss assumed that they were authentic words of Jesus) all made it clear that Jesus did not believe, as Ritschl assumed, that God's dominion would be established by the superior moral behavior of God's children, but would "come" or "be given" by an act of God.

The historical-critical work on the dominion of God in the proclamation of Jesus, begun by Johannes Weiss, continues to this day. It remains characteristic of all historical investigation. One tries to establish the best text of Jesus' teaching, and then, from all the sources available, one seeks to understand that teaching in terms of its historical context—at least that's where one starts. It sounds fairly simple; but in fact, in practice, it has proved to be very complicated.

Jesus Christ

Reactions to Johannes Weiss

Weiss's view, popularized in a slightly different form by Albert Schweitzer, met with very strong opposition. His interpretation of Jesus had such revolutionary implications that it was fought on every front. A professor of dogmatics in Berlin, Julius Kaftan, said: "If Johannes Weiss is right and the conception of the Kingdom of God is an eschatological one, then it is impossible to make use of this conception in dogmatics."[11] Think about it! A professor of theology saying that there is no room in his theological formulations for Jesus' view of the dominion of God, if Weiss's interpretation of it is correct. In other words, it doesn't make any difference *what* Jesus said, if Jesus' view is not consistent with mine! So where does theology get its foundations? Weiss's interpretation of Jesus was so dangerous to theology that theologians could find no place for it; so if Weiss is right, too bad for Jesus!

Now it is very interesting to discover that Julius Kaftan was finally convinced that Weiss *was* right, but that did not mean that Kaftan abandoned his theological principles. It was Jesus' view that had to be abandoned. But what happens to theology, and what happens to the faith of believers, if the preaching of Jesus is subject to rejection? Which is prior: Jesus' word or my construct? Wherein lies the authority of the Gospels if the words of Jesus have no authority—either Jesus' authentic words, or the words attributed to Jesus in the church by the Gospel authors? What can be the importance of trying to answer the historical question of what the person Jesus said, if, in any case, the words have no authority in the church and may be abandoned at will? These are major questions that the church must deal with.

Weiss's perception that Jesus held an apocalyptic view of the dominion of God produced a discontinuity between Jesus (and early Christian faith) and modern theology, and much theology was willing to dispose of its origins. Weiss himself, for example, did not attempt to bridge the gap between historical reality as he thought it to have been, and his own theology. He simply believed that we could no longer hold to the same view of the dominion that

Jesus held, since we no longer share Jesus' eschatological world view. So in the end Weiss took up precisely the same position as Ritschl's, which he had earlier attacked. And finally he confessed that his own conception of the dominion of God "parts company with Jesus' (view) at the most decisive point."

With Weiss, as with many theologians since Weiss, Jesus' words are usable if they do not conflict with one's own theological orientation. They are useful as validation, but not as norm. And the same becomes true, then, of the Gospels themselves. The fact that many different theological positions may be extracted from this or that verse of the Gospels means that one can usually find theological support of some kind there, if one looks hard enough. And many "lives of Jesus" have been written following that practice: seek out verses that support your presuppositions. Of course it is also true that in the end it must be acknowledged that the perceiver always plays a major role in relation to the perceived. One can never make definitive claims, but a detailed critical inquiry will certainly help in one's attempt at approximating the goal of finding the truth.

Johannes Weiss's investigations left him in the position of having no way to bridge the gap between Jesus' time and his own; he had no way to take what Jesus said about the dominion of God and apply it to his own life and times, to the church community in which he lived. He had no hermeneutical method by which to get from there to here.

What can scripture mean if it does not speak in any way to the contemporary church, if "at the decisive point" one must "part company with" what it says? Why should there be scripture readings in the Sunday service? Why would anyone read the Bible in daily devotions? If there is no way of relating biblical passages to one's own life and community, the Bible is irrelevant. To some people reading the Bible seems like entering a fantasy world, and one doesn't know what to make of it—how to read it, how to interpret it. The question involved here is the hermeneutical question, the question of how to listen to a first-century writing and hear it as though it were speaking today. Hermeneutics is the attempt to make relevant to one's own life and time a message or proclamation of a time gone by. It is also the attempt to interpret the ultimate significance of an event or of events of history long past. We must investigate now how it may be possible to understand in our time what Jesus intended by the term "dominion of God."

[5]

The Hermeneutics
of Rudolf Bultmann

If hermeneutics is the attempt, by one means or another, to hear and interpret for one's own time a message that was first delivered and heard at a much earlier time, or even centuries before, what hermeneutical method is available by which to understand an ancient message? Johannes Weiss did not have such a method, so the concept "dominion of God" was not usable to him. It had to remain locked in the past. He had no way of reading or listening to Jesus' words about the dominion of God that would permit him to believe that it had any relevance either to him or to the believers of his time. We come now to one of Weiss's students, Rudolf Bultmann.

Bultmann was for many years professor of New Testament at Marburg University, having succeeded his teacher Johannes Weiss. Bultmann also studied with Julius Kaftan in Berlin. He was not only the most influential New Testament scholar of his day, and perhaps of this century, but he was also one of the most provocative and challenging theologians of the first half of this century. He was not satisfied to study the New Testament simply out of an antiquarian interest—just to discover what was believed and written in the first two centuries of our era—and he disapproved of the liberal "peeling" practice by which one reduced the gospel to a small core. It was of supreme importance to Bultmann that he find a way to relate what he found in the New Testament to the life and faith of the church of his day, that he be able to interpret the significance of the preaching of Jesus and Paul and of other New Testament authors for his own time and place.

Weiss had pointed out that the expression "dominion of God"

had been used in theology as a kind of "floating" term, into which theologians (and particularly Ritschl) poured the meaning they would later extract, reminding one of the rabbit-in-the-hat trick. But after Weiss made the point that one must ask the historical-critical question of what Jesus meant by "dominion of God," and having answered that question to his own satisfaction, Weiss found that what Jesus had meant by the term was irrelevant to his own historical and existential situation. Jesus' Jewish apocalyptic view could not inform nineteenth-century theology. Apocalyptic eschatology could be understood *historically,* but it seemed to have no hermeneutical significance for theology in the modern world.

Then along came Weiss's pupil, Rudolf Bultmann. Bultmann agreed with his teacher that Jesus' view of the dominion of God was essentially that of Jewish apocalyptic. But, said Bultmann, Jesus was mistaken in thinking that the world was destined to come to an end *very soon.* His timetable was wrong. But before we discuss what this error meant to Bultmann, we must illuminate the hermeneutical method he worked out.

Bultmann followed a hermeneutics that he inherited, which understands it as "the art of understanding *expressions of life* (one German word) fixed in writing."[1] We will unpack this tightly worded definition.

Note, in the first place, that hermeneutics is said to be an "art" — not a science. "Art" is a broad term, not to be narrowly defined, having subjective, personal overtones. The second word in Bultmann's definition is "understanding": "the art of *understanding.*" "Understanding" is to be interpreted here in the widest possible terms; it does not refer merely to an activity of the mind. One may "understand" a mathematical equation; but one may also "understand" a child or a musical composition or a painting. When used in this latter sense, "understanding" includes opening oneself to what a person or object communicates, letting it have its *impact* on one. Of course the mind is involved in *all* understanding, but so are other "components" that contribute to the life of a human being. The model of the relationship between interpreter and text would be a dialogue.

The Hermeneutics of Rudolf Bultmann

Bultmann's definition refers next to "expressions of life." A text is only one form of "expression of life." What is true of a written text is true also of any form of human artistic expression: a quartet, an opera, a building, a sculpture, a painting, a dance, a poem, a novel, a play—all are "expressions of life." The latter three are also "fixed in writing," as are the Gospels, but a rock musical like *Hair* or *Godspell* is also an "expression of life."

Hair opened in New York City in 1967, during the Vietnam War. It made a very strong statement against that war. It was about the "flower people," the young people who were strongly opposed to the war in Vietnam and wanted the United States to get out of it. To be a participant in the theater during a performance of *Hair,* at the same time that the war against which the show was making such a strong statement was in progress, was a powerful experience. One had to open oneself to receive the words and music of *Hair,* and one was changed by the performance. One left the theater different from what one was before entering it. One did not need to inquire into its historical origins, with which one was very familiar.

But those who did not live through the period of the Vietnam War have a hard time understanding many people's intense feelings of disgust at America's involvement in that episode (most unusual in a time of war), and they have an equally hard time understanding what a performance of *Hair* meant in the sixties. When one went to witness and experience that musical during the war, one had to adopt a posture with regard to the strong message it conveyed. Most people attending a performance were probably sympathetic—they knew what they had come to see—but some undoubtedly found themselves in the wrong place. In any case, one was caught up in a dialogue with the musical, being either open to its passionate affirmations or hostile to them. It was impossible to remain neutral. To "understand" the musical one had to participate in it from where one sat. One participates in a dialogue with such a "text" with one's whole being, and not just with the mind.

When *Hair* was performed at a much later time, the viewer then had to make an inquiry into its historical origins (if one had not lived through that time), and one was interested in such questions as, Who wrote it? When? And where? And why? To try to enter into a performance of *Hair* at this later date, one would learn that it was written in the United States during the Vietnam War, and one would have to do research in the American history of the sixties and the circumstances that led to America's participation in that war. In other words, an understanding of *Hair* presupposes answers to historical-critical questions, but answers to those questions would not begin to exhaust the meaning and significance of the musical. When times changed, its message became more difficult to recapture; answers to the historical-critical questions became necessary, but alone failed to be very illuminating.

Yet *Hair* is not a *great* musical—it was time-bound, dependent for its understanding on a sharing of the life that produced it. A *great* work of art is not dated in the same way. It speaks to later generations as well as to the time in which it was created. Of course, in order to "receive" what it "says" one must ask critical questions of it, and one must come to know it. One must participate in a dialogue with it and allow it to have its impact, which, in turn, will change who one is. We will come back to this subject later, but let us return now to Bultmann's hermeneutics.

Bultmann agreed with Weiss that Jesus' view of the dominion of God was essentially that of Jewish apocalyptic. But, as we have seen, Bultmann believed that Jesus was mistaken in thinking that the world was destined to come to an end *very soon*. His timetable was in error. Nevertheless, Bultmann argued, with regard to hermeneutics it is not important that Jesus' chronology was off, though it is significant for the historical critic. Hermeneutics inquires about *expressions of life* disclosed in a text, so with regard to the dominion of God, it inquires about the understanding of human life expressed in the term. Hermeneutics is not interested in the accuracy of Jesus' predictions. And Bultmann argued that the understanding of human life disclosed in the Gospel texts may be valid, whether or not Jesus' chronology was correct. Jesus' proclamation of the dominion of God reveals Jesus' self-understanding and Jesus' understanding of existence; the accuracy of his chronology is not relevant to that understanding.

The Hermeneutics of Rudolf Bultmann

Bultmann offered a solution to the problem of the relation between historical criticism and hermeneutics. He bridged the gap between the ancient preacher and the modern preacher. By means of historical criticism he stated that Jesus adopted the apocalyptic mythology of his time; and then, by means of his understanding of hermeneutics, he viewed the text of Jesus' proclamation as an expression of Jesus' understanding of human life. What was important for Bultmann was not the precision of Jesus' predictions—not that objective fact—but the validity of Jesus' understanding of the world. The gap between Jesus and the modern interpreter, he said, is bridged because both want to come to an understanding of life in the world.

What, then, does Jesus' proclamation of the dominion of God reveal about Jesus' understanding of life? What is disclosed in the text? It is this, said Bultmann—that humankind is always, then and now, being confronted by the immediacy of God, is always being challenged to make a decision in light of that confrontation and relationship. The dominion of God is always "coming," always imminent—in Jesus' time and in ours.

This famous "demythologizing" proposal was directed at creating a way to move from the ancient text to the present time: one asks about the understanding of life hidden in the text, which is obscured by the mythological language in which it was expressed. So one "demythologizes" the text to interpret it correctly, to expose the understanding of life hidden there. To Bultmann that meant understanding the text existentially.

For Bultmann, mythological language is the language used to talk about the "other side" coming to "this side," the heavenly world impinging on the earthly world. The spatial metaphor presupposes the ancient cosmology: the heaven(s) is (are) above, earth is the flat surface under the heaven(s), and Sheol is the place under the earth where the dead are. To speak of God, in heaven, acting in some way on the earth is, for Bultmann, to speak mythologically. One uses language that describes a *human* activity and by analogy applies it to an activity of God. The language when used of God is, of course, inexact.

Jesus Christ

Bultmann understands the creation story in Genesis to be mythological: it speaks about God in heaven working on and creating what we know on this earth. The point of the language is not to tell us something about God—how God creates, how long it took God to create the world, in what order God created the various components of the universe, and so on; the point of mythological language is to tell human beings something about *themselves*. Thus the creation narrative tells human beings that, as they were created by God, they are and will always remain creatures utterly dependent upon God for their existence. Their posture before God is always the posture of the creature before the Creator. Mythological language is to be interpreted *existentially*. It is not to be eliminated, or peeled away, but is to be *interpreted*. Furthermore, it is not to be repeated as dogma and interpreted literally. It must be "demythologized." We will leave discussion of Bultmann now and return to his hermeneutics briefly in the next chapter.

[6]

Before Hermeneutics

Before the study of hermeneutics, before the adoption of a special means of reading an ancient literature in the modern day, many people simply read the Bible as a collection of factual statements, as truth from God delivered in propositional form. This is the Protestant biblicist way of reading scripture. The Bible is read as discursive prose, giving readers information about what they are to think and do, about what our universe is like. The Bible tells us how the world was created, and in what order, and how long the whole creative process took. It tells us where heaven is, where hell is, where angels live, how we are saved, and everything else we need to know for our salvation. The words of the Bible mean exactly what they say, and there is no need of finding a special way of reading them—there is no need for hermeneutics.

Take, for example, some sentences from Matthew's Sermon on the Mount, in the King James Version:

Take no thought for your life, what ye shall eat, or what ye shall drink; nor yet for your body, what ye shall put on. Is not the life more than meat, and the body than raiment? Behold the fowls of the air: for they sow not, neither do they reap, nor gather into barns; yet your heavenly Father feedeth them. Are ye not much better than they? Which of you by taking thought can add one cubit unto his stature? And why take ye thought for raiment? Consider the lilies of the field, how they grow; they toil not, neither do they spin: and yet I say unto you, That even Solomon in all his glory was not arrayed like one of these. Wherefore, if God so clothe the grass of the field, which to day is, and to morrow is cast into the oven, shall he not much more clothe you, O ye of little faith?

(Matt. 6:25–30)

Even in the seventeenth-century King James Version these words are perfectly understandable by literate people. Whether they can be *followed* is one question, but what they *say* is clear enough. One needs no training in critical analysis or in hermeneutics to read them, to know what they mean, and to love them. Of course the punctuation is not ours, nor all the spellings: "today" is now one word, so is "tomorrow"; we say "you" instead of "ye"; and our verb forms are different: the King James says "feedeth" rather than "feeds." "Behold" has unfortunately been abandoned in our day; we would say "they do not sow" rather than "they sow not," and we would translate the Greek verb as "clothed" rather than "arrayed." We would not say "*his* stature" when women are obviously as included in the words as men are; but none of these differences are enough to prevent, or to hinder in any way, our understanding. The words mean what they say, and are as intelligible to any layperson as they are to a priest or a New Testament professor.

The word "cubit" is not a widely used word, but anyone can easily discover its meaning by going to the dictionary. What the person who reads Greek will know, however, is that the word translated "stature" may also mean "age" or "length of life"; and that person could be a priest or layperson. The point is that there are words of the New Testament that are perfectly understandable without the use of any hermeneutical method.

But that is not by any means always the case. Often, in fact, the problem of how to understand looms large. How does one read Mark 13, for example? What does one make of such words as:

> the sun will be darkened
>   and the moon will not give its light,
>   and the stars will be falling from heaven,
>   and the powers in the heavens will be shaken.
> (Mark 13:24–25)

Before Hermeneutics

Are they to be read just like all other words—whether scriptural or not—just like the words quoted above from Matthew? The biblicist would say that indeed they are to be read literally, that they say what they mean to say, and are true. The biblicist would continue that we have in Mark 13 a prediction of what is to happen at the end; at the end time one is to look for the occurrence of these events in the sky, and if they do occur, one will know that the end of history is imminent.

That is the way the biblicist reads all words of the Bible—they are propositions that are to be taken literally. But some major problems accompany this way of reading scripture. In the first place, it has no way to explain inconsistencies in the biblical narratives: the inconsistencies in the Genesis stories of creation, the inconsistencies in the various Gospels' reports of what Jesus said and did. More importantly, biblicists remove the Bible from the possibility of all historical or literary criticism. The Bible is not classified as another form of literature, and is not to be studied the way literature is studied. One is not to investigate the meaning of scripture by employing the canons of criticism used in studying all other literature.

This means that one cannot arrive at one's own understanding of scripture, because it is not to be read the way any other literature is read. So one must be *told* what the Bible means; one must go to the pastor who is initiated into the mysteries of its meaning. Therefore enormous power resides in the hands of the biblical interpreter, who tells others who the "beast" is in the book of Revelation, and unravels all other biblical mysteries.

In the early part of this century another way of reading scripture was opened to the believer, and that was the academic way of the so-called liberals, or "modernists," who viewed all biblical language in general with considerable skepticism. To them the language of scripture was all dated, and *not* true: there are no such places as heaven and hell—we know that now; Jesus was not a divine being—there are no such beings—but Jesus was a very good man whose example and some of whose teaching remain valuable to the human race. Most ordinary believers assumed that the words of scripture meant what they said, but if they were educated, they might often begin to have more and more doubts about the Bible's relevance. Liberals provided a different way of reading scripture that did not make exhorbitant demands on the rational believer, but that did require education and study. When "liberals" came to the words of Mark 13, they often dealt with them simply by not re-marking about them at all. They could just observe that the words "were taken from the Old Testament," and that if the words were intended to describe "objective phenomena," they were not be-lievable. The liberal interpreter could say that the predictions of Mark 13 were at one time understood as forecasts of occurrences yet to take place, and were acceptable to people who believed that the world was flat, that the heavens were up, and that God could instigate such happenings as Mark describes any time God chose. Then the liberal would continue that now we know better, and we no longer look for such catastrophes in the sky. The words are primitive and quaint, but have no meaning for the modern, scien-tifically educated man or woman.

The liberal believed that one could accept as true only state-ments that conform to known scientific laws. The result of this be-lief was that experiences and events described in the Bible were psychologized, or interpreted as incorrect scientific propositions handed down from "primitive" times; they were read and inter-preted through modern lenses that were unknown in the ancient world. The liberal would ask the rhetorical question, What *really* happened? and then would answer out of his or her own magnifi-cent wisdom. What the early disciples "saw" after the resurrection, for example, was interpreted in terms of categories the disciples knew nothing about, and in terms of those categories, what they "saw" was repudiated. By means of a modern, arbitrarily selected lens, the truth of the disciples' experiences was denied.

But when you view other people's experiences through your own glasses, and make no attempt to view them through theirs — which may be very different from yours — how adequate is your ex-planation of them? Are you in fact talking about the same thing? Should not the modern interpreter, rather, try to discover the ancient lens of the people involved, and try to look through that? How helpful and reliable is a hermeneutical method that brings modern categories to bear on ancient experiences and events, and then interprets them in terms that would not have been understandable at the time they occurred? That is one of the great weaknesses of the "liberal" hermeneutics — it bypasses the testimony of the participants in events long past, and replaces it with one's own reconstruction of it. It fails to "see" what was "seen," and implicitly accuses the original participants of having misinterpreted the "facts."

The liberals were intellectuals who were viewed by conservatives as trying to destroy the faith of poor, not-too-bright Christians, but their interpretation of scripture never filtered down very pervasively into the churches, where rank and file Christians intuited that there was something wrong with it, somewhere. The "liberal" hermeneutics remained the discourse of the relatively few who were professional scholars. In fact, it is still generally true that *any* hermeneutical method of reading scripture, most unfortunately, remains largely confined to the classrooms and studies of faculties and students of theological seminaries and college departments of religion, and their interchanges with each other. The use of a hermeneutical method of any kind requires what is sometimes believed to be too much study for the average believer to engage in, especially without the help and encouragement of a trained pastor or teacher; and the average minister seems to believe that too much teaching skill and too much time and preparation are required to provide such help to lay people.

There was a second weakness in the modernist interpretation: it turned out that much of the Bible was read as though it were ancient fantasy and had nothing to do with faith. In New Testament studies it developed that only a small core of the New Testament was relevant to faith — mostly certain carefully selected words of Jesus; but most of the New Testament was interpreted as first-century embellishment of the simple teachings of Jesus that was no longer usable in the church. It had to be peeled away to get at the core. But the small core that remained was inadequate to account for the power of the faith that had brought the church into being, and was totally inadequate as a basis for the daily life of a believer.

Another kind of peeling away is evident also in the work of the recent Jesus Seminar. After years of study, and multiple research papers passed back and forth among the participants, the seminar finally revealed that very little of what the Gospels offer as words from Jesus are actually Jesus' words. What is implied in that judgment? That the words the Jesus Seminar printed in red are more valuable to the church than words printed in other colors? That they are truer? That, coming from Jesus, they are more authoritative, or more "divine"? That the church should pay more attention to them than it does to the rest of the Gospels or to the rest of the New Testament? But the church has never believed that the Gospels have a higher place in the canon than, say, Paul, or that words designated as "authentic" words of Jesus are truer and of more value to the church than other words of the Gospels. So what is the significance *for the life and faith of the church* in the distinctions worked out so laboriously by the Jesus Seminar?

Certainly their investigations have significance for historical studies, and their conclusions are to be set alongside the results of the investigations of others. To determine as best one can which words in the Gospels were actually spoken by Jesus is helpful in interpreting their meaning, but does not give them a special status in the Gospels, higher than that of other words. It is the Gospels that were canonized, not the words of Jesus. So the question remains: What is the relevance *for the life and faith of the church* of distinctions made between words of Jesus and other words in the Gospels? What is of supreme importance in the *church* is the witness to Jesus Christ found in the Gospels, and in Paul's letters, and in the rest of the New Testament.

Until Rudolf Bultmann came along, the two major alternative ways of interpreting scripture that were available to the church were the way of the biblicist and the way of the "liberal." Johannes Weiss took the second way, and all fundamentalists still choose the first. Though they employ critical methods to read other literature, for fundamentalists the Bible is off limits with regard to criticism. The words say what they mean, and if one doesn't understand them, one asks the pastor what their meaning is. The pastor will tell you what a difficult text means. The pastor has the knowledge and the authority.

In my own early life these were the only two ways I knew. But then Bultmann came along, and he provided me—and a whole generation and more of believers—with a hermeneutical method of getting from the text to current life that was very different from the way of the modernist, who reduced the gospel to less and less. Bultmann said that we cannot accept what he called the "mythology" of the New Testament as dogma (rejecting the biblicist view); but he also said that neither can we eliminate all New Testament "mythology" as irrelevant to contemporary faith, peeling away everything but the core (rejecting the liberal view). What we must do, he said, is *interpret* the mythology, and recapture its original meaning for faith. As we saw in the last chapter, this is to be done by "demythologizing" (a word coined by Bultmann) the text. Recall now his hermeneutical principle: one asks about the "understanding of life" disclosed in the text.

Bultmann believed that the mythology of the New Testament is dead, that its symbolic language no longer fulfills its evocative function. So he tried to translate the mythology as an "expression of life" and found a way do that hermeneutically by demythologizing. His way of interpreting remains an option open to all those for whom the biblical myths are now dead and nonevocative.

Let us look now at Psalm 137:1 and ask Bultmann's question of it: what expression of life is implied in that text? Psalm 137:1 reads: "By the rivers of Babylon—there we sat down and there we wept when we remembered Zion." What would a critical analysis of that verse tell us? We have some idea, though we cannot be sure, about what was the historical context of this psalm. It would make very good sense to suppose that it was written by a person who had returned from Babylonian exile in 538 B.C.E., and who in this verse is remembering the horrendous experience of being in Babylon, bereft of Jerusalam and the temple.

But a dialogue with that psalm opens up large vistas of meaning and understanding that go far beyond any light that historical criticism can shed on it. One does not understand that psalm simply as a historical record of the experience of a Jewish person who lived over two thousand years ago. The historical context does not control the interpretation of the text. But what is the "expression of life" contained in it? We transfer the scene. We read our scene into it. We enter into dialogue with the psalmist and his or her situation, and let the psalm have its impact on our lives. The results of our historical-critical inquiry give way to our existential dialogue with the psalm.

But the use and relevance of the text for us does not end there. The composer Giuseppe Verdi made a political witness in much of his music. It happens that northern Italy, including Milan—an important city for Verdi's life—was subject to Austria until Garibaldi succeeded in uniting an independent Italy. And during this time of Austrian domination, Verdi wrote his early opera *Nabucco,* which contains a glorious and very famous choral prayer, reflecting this verse of the 137th psalm. In this choral prayer Jews in exile mourn for their independence. In the opera, the prayer reflects not a Jewish situation of exile in the early sixth century B.C.E., but an early nineteenth-century Italian longing for independence. Verdi has disguised that Italian longing by referring to a similar yearning recounted in the psalm. He has illuminated the situation of his time in Italy by referring back to scripture that had grown out of Babylon's oppression of the Jews two thousand years earlier.

When we listen to Verdi's great *Nabucco* chorus, the prayer sung there is ostensibly being sung by Jews being oppressed in Babylon in the sixth century B.C.E., but in actuality it reflects Austrian oppression in northern Italy in the time of Verdi. Yet when we hear the chorus now, it has little to do with either the Jews being oppressed in Babylon or with Verdi's situation in Italy; rather we have our own dialogue with Verdi's words and music, and we let them have their impact on us, on our own contemporary lives.

We read or hear the words of Psalm 137:1 just as Verdi did; we appropriate them and take them to our own life and times in the same way that Verdi did. We let the words have their impact on us; we have a dialogue with them; we listen to them, and we ask them questions, and they speak to us again.

[7]

Metaphor

Before we go directly to the subject of the meaning of the expression "dominion of God" in Jesus' preaching, we should say something about different kinds of language and how each of them works. As metaphor is a major characteristic of all language, shedding light on how one interprets "dominion of God" as well as much other scriptural language, we will take some time to discuss metaphors and what metaphors accomplish.

A metaphor is not simply a grammatical matter, as many of us were taught in school. In school we learned that the statement "An airplane is like a bird" is a simile; but if we take out the "like," and say, "An airplane is a bird," we have a metaphor. But this strictly grammatical distinction between a "metaphor" and a "simile" does not begin to illuminate the special means of communication for which metaphors are used.

Metaphors have been defined in many different ways, and there is nothing resembling universal agreement about what "metaphor" means and how metaphors work. I will describe "metaphor" as used in this discussion with the following very brief definition: A metaphor extends meaning through comparison and juxtaposition. The juxtaposition creates the tension found in all metaphorical language.

If I say, "Life is a dream," the character of dreams is ascribed to life, and so the meaning of "life" is extended. Of course, life *is not* a dream; the statement "life is a dream" cannot be interpreted literally, as a proposition. The juxtaposition of "dreams" with "life" creates the metaphorical tension.

Jesus Christ

Another metaphor: In the statement "God is our Father," the character of fatherhood is ascribed to God, so extending the meaning of the word "God." God *is not literally* our father—I know who my father is; but the juxtaposition of "God" with "father" creates the tension. When it was first said that "God is Father," the statement must have elicited considerable shock and wonder. What an amazing way to think of God—as *Father*! But that statement does not seem very amazing anymore. By repetition, the dissimilarities, "God" and "Father," gradually disappear, and the similarities become more and more taken for granted, until the statement fails to evoke any response at all. The dissimilars have become similar. We no longer have a metaphor; instead we have a proposition. The metaphor, repeated over and over again, becomes a symbol, and by repeated usage the symbol dies.

In a metaphor we have what Aristotle called "an intuitive perception of the similarities in dissimilars." Repeated often enough, however, metaphors become clichés. Our language is full of dead clichés that had their beginnings as interesting, evocative metaphors, in which dissimilars were intuited as similar. Take, for example, the expression, "a warm reception," where an adjective having to do with temperature is joined to a dissimilar—a reception. When the metaphor was first used it must have elicited some interest, the word "warm" not being used in its literal sense of "moderate heat," but taking on a metaphorical, nonliteral meaning. It provided a new way of seeing a reception. Now, however, the expression is no longer even vaguely interesting, and provides no new insight at all. It would be stricken out by a red pencil in any writing class. Through repetition, it has become a cliché.

A primitive person will use the word "run" of a lion—a lion "runs" when it moves quickly from one place to another. It runs, literally. But if the word "run" is subsequently applied to *water*— "water runs"—it is used in a new context, not literally, but metaphorically. What is known in one connection (that lions run) is applied to another (the movement of water), allowing the hearer to perceive water in a new way—as though underneath the water's surface there were little legs propelling the water along quickly from one place to another.

Metaphor

Later it was said that a car "runs," and a new metaphor was created. Dissimilars were juxtaposed. It is also said that a watch "runs." But, of course, those dissimilars are now similar, and in all these cases we have "dead" metaphors. The metaphors have become propositions. A verb originally applied to leg movement was juxtaposed to objects having no legs. New metaphors were born, only to die and become mere descriptive statements of fact.

"Airplanes are birds"; "police officers are pigs"; "God is our Father"—they are all metaphors. "Birds," "pigs," and "Father," all known in one context, are used as "screens" by which, or through which, to know someone else. "Father" is a screen, or lens, through which God is viewed. The screen is, of course, inexact, just as inexact as it is in the metaphor "police officers are pigs." Police officers are certainly not pigs, but the metaphor is intended to throw a negative light on the police, and asks the hearer of the metaphor to view the police through the lens of "pigs." In this metaphor, what is the connotation of "pig"? How are police officers viewed? To those who raise pigs the metaphor is probably not pejorative, but the connotation will vary with each person who hears it. A metaphor is a most inexact way of speaking, and what it says depends for its meaning on the person who hears or reads it.

That is exactly the situation with the metaphor "God is our Father." "Father" is the screen through which "God" is viewed. The screen does not describe literally or exactly, and it will connote different things to different people. We all bring our creative imaginations to it. To those who have known and loved their fathers, the metaphor will work; but to those who have not known fathers, or who have been terrified by them, the metaphor will not work.

I realize that for some people the statement "God is Father" is not understood as a metaphor, but is interpreted as a statement of fact about God: God *is* our Father, and we must call God "Father." One also hears it said frequently that "Father" was what Jesus called God, and that Jesus' disciples should do the same. I can only respond in this brief chapter by pointing out that there is a long tradition, going back to the early church, which holds that God does not have a name, *any* name.[1] And in spite of what one often reads, there is no certain evidence that Jesus always or even often called God "Father."[2]

But if "Father" used for God is a metaphor, as I believe it is, it is also true that the metaphor has become so overused that it is now hardly evocative at all, except for those who do not like the screen, for whom this metaphor has a highly negative connotation. For all people who have never known a loving father, the "Our Father" of Jesus' prayer simply cannot be said. For them, the use of "Father" for God is impossible, and hearing others call God "Father" is disturbing or even painful. That metaphor represents to them an absent, or oppressive, or abusive parent. Like all metaphors, it works very differently with different people. It does not have an exact meaning, but its meaning varies with the individuals who hear it.

Now if one were to say, "God is our Mother," the power of that metaphor would be apparent. To put up the screen of "mother" through which to view God would elicit the response of a true metaphor. So one can begin to understand the power of the "God is our Father" metaphor when it was first heard: "Like as a father pitieth his children, so the Lord pitieth them that fear him" (Ps. 103:13, KJV).

While metaphors are imprecise and open-ended, and have many different meanings, they are not replaceable. A metaphor does not make a statement that is literally true, but it functions as a screen through which something is illuminated. The imprecision of the metaphor is evident. If I say, for example, "John flipped," what do I mean? Do I mean that he showed some surprise, or that he almost passed out? Or am I speaking literally about a dive he made from a diving board?

Many current metaphors in English are taken over from the language of electronics: we "plug into" somebody; or we "read" her, as in a graph; or we say that a person is not "wired right." These are all metaphors. None of them is intended literally; all of them are inexact. They are also difficult for foreigners to understand and are usually untranslatable. What would they mean in societies that do not have wires and plugs? Something of the same problem arises with the "God as Father" metaphor for a person who has not known a father, or who has not had a good father. But we have to live with the imprecison of the metaphor because there is no other way to get at the principal subject directly. And this means—because there is no way to get at the subject directly—that metaphors are not embellishments or ornaments. They are not dispensable. There is absolutely no other way to say what they say.

When one hears or reads a metaphor, one has no way to perceive the new insight apart from the metaphor itself. The insight is communicated precisely *in* the metaphor. Any attempt to paraphrase the metaphor reveals that the metaphor is inseparable from what is being said. One person cannot tell another what a metaphor "means." It means what it says, and what it says will vary with the person who hears it.

A good poet, by using the familiar in an unfamiliar context, creates a metaphor that "works," and so opens our eyes; it not only helps us *see,* but at the same time provides us with a new *experience.* By seeing something new, we become something different.

Read the following lines from Denise Levertov's "Mass for the Day of St. Thomas Didymus." In the "Agnus Dei" she writes:

> What terror lies concealed
> in strangest words, *O lamb of God that taketh away*
> *the Sins of the World:* an innocence
>   smelling of ignorance,
>   born in bloody snowdrifts,
>   licked by forebearing
> dogs more intelligent than its entire flock put together?[3]

The metaphorical language "works." It does not speak directly; its meaning changes with different readings; it is elaborated in many ways. So one is led to see something new, to have a new experience, and to become, to that degree, something different.

When Louis Armstrong was asked, "What's so great about jazz?" he would answer, "If you have to ask, I don't know." In other words, I can't talk about it with you unless you already understand it. The point is the same with Denise Levertov's lines, and with all biblical metaphors. One has to be able to "tune in" to them, and to know what they are pointing to. And so it is also with any great work of art, as with the object of one's faith. Perception is very personal and cannot be totally explained. "If you have to ask, I don't know."

One further point: It is not the case that there is only one "right" metaphor, and that all others are "wrong." In that case, all metaphors but one would be superfluous. Metaphors do not "correspond" to what is. They just seem to fit, or are appropriate to our experience, providing a fresh way of perceiving.

What we are talking about is various ways of seeing—there are many different ways. No words exist that correspond exactly to "what is," and there is certainly no word that begins to correspond to what "God" is. The metaphor *is* the thing—it is a special access we have to the "thing."

We are all deficient in awareness, very deficient. We do not "see" many things; in fact, we have a remarkable ability to screen out most things that might otherwise come within our purview. T. S. Eliot wrote in "Burnt Norton":

> Go, go, go, said the bird: human kind
> Cannot bear very much reality.[4]

Many years ago a very good friend of mine who lived in Bar Harbor, Maine, phoned me one evening and told me that his wife, Lee, who for many years had had a heart problem, was suffering an attack and needed attention. He asked me whether I thought he should take her to the local hospital, which was quite small, or whether he should drive her to Bangor, about 45 minutes away. I said I would phone my doctor and get his advice. The doctor told me that he would take her to the local hospital where she could get immediate care, and I relayed that advice to my friend.

The next day I decided to drive to Bar Harbor and see how Lee was getting along. I had driven there many times before during the summer, but I had never seen a sign for the Bar Harbor hospital, and had no idea where in the world it was. So I launched out, thinking that when I got to Bar Harbor I could inquire of someone where the hospital was.

Metaphor

When I came to a major fork in the road where signs tell you which road to take to Bar Harbor, I saw for the first time in my life a small blue sign with an arrow, and "To Hospital" printed on it. Subsequently, every time I came to a juncture of any kind I saw the same signs—not a single one of which I had ever noticed before. And I drove straight to the hospital, following signs all the way. They had always been invisible to me.

We screen out most of what we might otherwise see, including terrible horrors which, if we really saw them, we could not ever take in. It is the function of all art, including all great literature, to help create awareness of what is, from which we are so largely cut off. And metaphor, including metaphorical religious language, is a special linguistic tool by which literature may create this awareness.

Philip Wheelwright tells a Zen Buddhist story of a student who asked his Japanese Zen teacher: "If the Buddha is more than Siddhartha Gotama, who lived many centuries ago, then tell me, please, what is the real nature of Buddha?"

The teacher replied: "The blossoming branch of a plum tree."

The pupil supposed that the teacher had not heard his question, so he said: "What I asked, worthy Sir, and what I am eager to know is, What is Buddha?"

The teacher replied: "A pink fish with golden fins swimming idly through the blue sea."

The pupil, now somewhat confused, said, "Will not your Reverence tell me what Buddha is?"

The teacher replied: "The full moon cold and silent in the night sky, turning the dark meadow to silver."[5]

This anecdote simply illustrates that the answer to the conundrum "What is Buddha?" is of little significance. What is important is an awareness of the heart and mind to reality, to as much of what is as one can take in. And metaphor helps us in this seeing. In fact, metaphor is *required* for this seeing to take place.

[8]

Signs, Images, and Symbols

In the Western world, ever since the French philosopher René Descartes (1596–1650), it has been held that only scientific precision in language can represent the truth, and further, that language is able to represent the truth exactly. But in more recent times it has been realized that precise language cannot express much of what is important to say. Philip Wheelwright refers to scientific language as "block language," or *steno language,* to which he contrasts "fluid language," or *tensive language.*[1] Closely corresponding to Wheelwright's categories are what Paul Tillich calls "signs" (i.e., steno language) and "symbols" (i.e., tensive language).[2]

Steno language, or signs, bear roughly a one-to-one relationship to what they represent. They are univocal. The mathematical sign *pi,* for example, has a very specific denotation: it always denotes the ratio of the circumference of a circle to its diameter. The letter *B* in textual studies always represents the Greek manuscript Vaticanus. *Pi* and *B* are steno symbols, or what Tillich would call "signs." "Circle" and "square" and "chair" and "sky"—all are words that have precise, long-established, univocal meanings. Everyone knows exactly what they mean, and they are easily translated into the corresponding words of other languages. Since Descartes many people have held that only this kind of language can communicate meaning, but throughout most of human history no one would have assumed that steno language is the only language that can speak truth.

Tensive language, or what Tillich calls symbols, on the other hand, is characteristic of poetry, as well as Jesus' parables and Jesus' concept of the "dominion of God." In fact, tensive language is characteristic of theology in general. In tensive language there is always some semantic tension. If no such tension is there, the language is nonpoetic, and mostly cerebral. Recall the verse from Shelley's poem "To Night":

> Wrap thy form in a mantle gray,
> Star-inwrought!
> Blind with thine hair the eyes of Day;
> Kiss her until she be wearied out,
> Then wander o'er city, and sea, and land,
> Touching all with thine opiate wand—
> Come, long-sought![3]

What do these words mean? They contain much semantic tension created by the juxtaposition of the "night," "form," and "mantle"; or the juxtaposition of "night" and "hair," or of "night" and "kiss," or "night" and "wander" and "touching." Does night have "hair"? Does it "kiss" or "wander"? The language is very inexact, and an exact meaning is impossible to determine. But is it meaningless? Read as steno language, none of it can be true; so we have to read it differently, and allow the words to say something other than what they would mean in ordinary prose.

Or consider A. E. Housman's line:

> White in the moon the long road lies.[4]

The tension here is found in the juxtaposition of "moonlight" with "road." The language is, strictly speaking, inaccurate and very vague. Is the road made of dirt, or tar, or macadam? *Where* is the road—does it wind through a forest, or does it lead straight through a field? How high is the moon? How bright? Is it full, or is it a new moon? Is it wintertime and is there snow on the ground? What is imaged is not determined—only the barest outline. The imagination of each reader supplies the details.

Tensive language is about a unique experience that may never have taken place before. Nonpoetic language, or steno language, on the other hand, is about what is publicly known and generally shared: "two plus two equals four"; "it is cold in winter in Maine." Of course steno language requires some interpretation, just as tensive language does. Steno language is on a continuum with tensive language, but the latter has no semantic tension. Steno language speaks directly; but tensive language or symbolic language speaks indirectly, evoking feelings and meanings larger than literal statements can convey. Philip Wheelwright defines a symbol as follows: "A symbol, in general, is a relatively stable and repeatable element of perceptual experience, standing for some larger meaning or set of meanings which cannot be given, or not fully given, in perceptual experience itself."[5] Furthermore, one is not always sure what is intended by such image language.

Images

Speaking of image language, let us think for a moment about what an image is. An image points to the most concrete element of poetic or religious language. Imagistic language is a major component of human speaking. Images not only describe; they also give hints or suggestions, and lead the mind into wider pastures, different for each person. Children's language is replete with images: castles, witches, princes, princesses, giants, fairies, elves, dragons—all are images. They evoke feelings as well as ideas; and, above all, they evoke the imagination. They do not describe exactly, but they carry with them many associations, private associations not shared by others.

If one draws a picture of a castle, and shows the drawing to a child, the child will probably find fault with it, because the child holds a different image of what a castle is. The child will say, "But you forgot the moat"; or "the moat is too wide"; or "you don't have any turrets." And the child will have many other criticisms. What a castle is, if it is used as an image and is not intended literally, is not known exactly. It has no precise definition. Can one say that images do not convey truth because they are inexact? Ask a child.

Symbols

Just like a metaphor or image, a symbol is inexact; and like them it evokes feelings and the imagination, and leads the mind into broader places than the symbol itself denotes. A symbol evokes something of the wonder and mystery of the world. This is what Wallace Stevens was referring to when he wrote:

Signs, Images, and Symbols

The poem must resist the intelligence
Almost successfully. . . .[6]

The difference between a sign and a symbol is sometimes obscure. It depends on the perceiver or hearer to determine whether one is dealing with a sign or a symbol. Take, for example, our national flag. Sometimes the American flag functions simply as a sign or steno symbol for the nation. It has a univocal reference—namely, the United States. Where the flag is, there is the country it represents. The flag then functions like a mathematical sign. We may see the flag on top of a post office building, or in a corner of a church, but we will probably not notice it at all. And if we do see it, it will not create any feelings, and the imagination will not be called into play. A sign elicits no elation, no joy, no excitement. It is nonevocative.

But if the flag is raised at the Olympics, and the national anthem is being played for an American who has just won a gold medal, the flag may function for an American in the stands as a real symbol. There will be many non-Americans present for whom it will fail to evoke any reaction at all—or, perhaps, it will evoke only a negative reaction, and the reaction among Americans will also vary greatly in degree and in kind. But for some people present, the slow raising of the flag will be highly evocative.

What images will the flag evoke? The answer to that question will depend wholly on the person who perceives it. Symbols do not evoke specific images—they evoke as many different images, or clusters of images, as there are individuals responding to it. If an American is very far from home—at an Olympics game, for instance—and the flag is raised, it may evoke remembrance of things back home in America that one is missing, like hamburgers and milk shakes. Or it may evoke the memory of a spouse, or child, or friend who, because of illness, could not attend the games. A whole cluster of images will be elicited, which will vary with the perceiver. *What* is evoked by a symbol is always undetermined, but if something functions as a real symbol, it will be evocative, unspecifically evocative. That is how symbols work.

What finally happens to a symbol, however, is that through usage, through familiarity, it loses its symbolic power, and it functions then only as a sign or steno symbol. Its power evaporates. The flag of the American colonies began its history as a powerful symbol during the Revolutionary War. It was carried into battle and summoned the soldiers who followed it to fight with their lives. But with familiarity and the constant presence of the flag in public places, it has largely lost its symbolic power. That symbolic power may, however, return to the symbol *if it is used in a new context.* Hence its potentially evocative power at the Olympics.

Another example of a symbol whose power is often lost is the cross. For most of the time, probably, the cross functions simply as a sign, a steno symbol, whose power is largely dissipated. It is usually nonevocative, and so its enormous significance in the New Testament writings of the first-century church largely escapes us. What is required, if the power of the cross is to be restored, is a new context in which to appear. The late Dean Inge once wrote: "It is the tendency of all symbols to petrify or evaporate, and either process is fatal to them."[7]

It is not easy to restore symbolic power to symbols that have degenerated into signs. A poet, or a great theologian or preacher, is able to reperceive the symbol in a new way—from a new angle, in a new context—and restore its symbolic power. Significant language in one generation becomes a tired body of dead clichés in the next. The language of Paul and John, when it first appeared, was highly metaphorical, able to create new insights in its hearers and readers. Today, when that same language is read, it may be so familiar that it raises not the smallest stir of the heart. It falls heavy on the ear, and fails to engage the mind or the imagination. No sparks are created; the symbolic power of the words is gone.

Like poetry, religious language requires real symbols if it is to succeed in eliciting the necessary imaginative response, or cluster of images, in the listener, and so disclose what we might call *presence* in a new, imaginative way. Let us look at the presence that symbols evoke.

Signs, Images, and Symbols

Presence is always a mystery. It claims our awe and our gratitude. A "thing" is characterized by spatiotemporal and causal relations with other things: we ask about its name, its function, its relation to other things, the place where it may be found, and so on. But as Dean Inge said: "Everything, in being what it is, is symbolic of something more."[8]

One's world may be enlarged when one views a rainbow, or a sunset, or a garden of flowers in the rain—when one confronts presence. And the fact that one person may feel presence and another person may not, in the same place and under exactly the same circumstances, indicates that the experience has been made possible by one's personal history, which is unique and cannot be duplicated in any other person. That is why a simple matter cannot be communicated in a simple way.

Once when I was in Paris, I came out of a store onto a typically beautiful, wide Parisian boulevard. I looked up and saw two complete rainbows. That was the only time in my life I have seen two rainbows at the same time. The sight took my breath away. At the end of that boulevard, two rainbows! I stopped walking immediately, and just stared. And I could not help but notice that I was the only person staring. All the other people went on about their business as though nothing remarkable was to be seen. But I felt a presence. I was overjoyed. The world was a beautiful place—two rainbows in spectacular Paris! I was invigorated, and was reminded again of the presence of God.

An object is always an object to a *subject*. What something is— a rainbow, a sunset—is what it is *to* someone. There are no objects apart from subjects. An object is not something in itself, with its own meaning, but it is an object in relation to a subject; so what it is, and what it means, depends on who the subject is who perceives it. Further, what it is includes a presence—a new thing that is more than the sum of me and the rainbow. It is that new presence that affects my "world," the sphere in which I live my life. My "world" is not the same as anybody else's "world."

But to communicate to someone else what may have been a very simple experience to me—two rainbows in Paris, a sunset in the western sky—requires that I give some signals, some helps to understanding, some indirect guidance. The great gift of poets is, in part, that they can talk around the subject, offering suggestions indirectly so as to awaken an appropriate response in the hearer. To speak directly would negate the possibility of evoking a response. It is not different with the preacher or theologian. Both must speak indirectly, all of which makes the writing of sermons or theology so immensely difficult. Without some direction, readers or hearers may draw too much on their own subjective imaginations, and so fail to come to an understanding of the picture the preacher or theologian is trying to convey; but the direction must be subtle, and give only hints.

Gertrude Stein, who was an extraordinary writer and human being, occasionally failed as a poet. She once wrote the line, "Pigeons on the grass alas." Speaking about the line later on the radio, she said, "That's exactly how I felt about it." But to state exactly how she felt about it was not to convey anything at all about the experience. She needed to speak about it indirectly, and give only hints about her experience. She said too much, and thus nothing at all. Her experience was not communicated by the simple repetition of that brief phrase, for it was not evocative. There was no semantic tension in her utterance, no symbolic power.

Verbal communication is extraordinarily difficult and complex. It cannot be accomplished by direct language, by the use of simple steno symbols. The trick is to find the appropriate nonliteral language. In poetic and religious communication, including sermons, the simple repetition of a simple experience is not adequate to elicit a response in someone else. Tensive symbols are required—an evocative image, a metaphor, or the revitalization of a familiar symbol. The simple repetition of an old symbol has a deadening effect on hearers and readers.

[9]

Myth, Symbol, and Dominion of God

As with other words used to talk about various kinds of language, the definition of "myth" varies according to its interpreters. We have already noted the way in which Bultmann uses the word. Mythological language for him is language that talks about "the other side" as it relates to "this side," or any language that focuses on the entry by the heavenly world into the affairs of this world.[1]

Philip Wheelwright's understanding of myth is rather different. He quotes Alan Watts's definition of myth as follows: "Myth is to be defined as a complex of stories—some no doubt fact, and some fantasy—which, for various reasons, human beings regard as demonstrations of the inner meaning of the universe and of human life."[2]

In the Old Testament there are two kinds of myth that have been woven together. There is the ancient myth of creation, which Israel took over from the Canaanites, to which the myth of God as King is related. There are also the myths that tell of the history of God's redemption of Israel, which include Israel's understanding of its deliverance from Egypt, of its conquest of Canaan, of David's taking of the Ark to Zion, and of Solomon's building of the Temple. That history functioned in Israel as a collection of myths about God acting as King, which Israel regarded as "demonstrations of the inner meaning of the universe and of human life."[3] Israel's belief in the myth of God acting as their King led to the introduction in Israel of the symbol "kingdom of God." That symbol depended for its meaning on the myth.

Jesus Christ

Dominion of God
as Symbol

When Jesus spoke of the "dominion of God," as according to the Gospels he often did, what did he mean by the term? To what was he referring? What connotations did the expression have in his mind, and what connotations did it evoke in his hearers? Let me suggest that "dominion of God" in Jesus' preaching was an extended metaphor, or a symbol. It evoked a world that was God's world, and it shed light on that world by being used in different contexts and illustrated by various stories and parables.

Let us begin this discussion of the dominion of God in Jesus' proclamation by noting that, according to the Gospel of Mark, Jesus said that "no *sign* will be given to this generation" (Mark 8:12). If you look at the Gospels in parallel form[4] you will see that both Matthew and Luke, who knew and used Mark's Gospel, have Jesus add something to what he said in Mark. Both Gospels have Jesus say—and Matthew, in fact, has Jesus say twice—that no sign will be given to this generation "except the sign of Jonah." And then both Matthew and Luke go on to explain, in different ways, what the "sign of Jonah" meant.

On historical-critical grounds, it seems very likely that Mark has recorded Jesus' words accurately, and that as the quotation of Jesus' words was handed down, the except clause ("except the sign of Jonah") was added to it, unexplained. Then later on, when Matthew and Luke incorporated Jesus' words into their Gospels, each writer independently added an interpretation of what the phrase meant.

We should also note in passing that the usual English translation of Mark 8:12, "no sign will be given," may not be adequate. It is very possible that Mark's Greek assumes a previous, unwritten statement or imprecation. The Greek word NRSV translates "no" usually means "if." If it is translated "if," the literal translation of Mark would be, "Truly I tell you, *if a sign will be given to this generation,*" with the main clause missing. If we supply a main clause it might go something like this: "[I would be quite mistaken, or May something happen to me] *if* a sign will be given to this generation." No except clause could possibly be added to such a rigorous rejection of any sign whatever. Hence it happens that both Matthew and Luke, who have the except clause, drop the word in Mark that implies the curse (the word translated "if"), and substitute for it a Greek negative corresponding to the English "no" or "not." Matthew and Luke do not presuppose a previous main clause that may well have been assumed by the author of Mark, and both have changed the "if" to a simple negative: *"no sign will be given."*

In any case, in both Mark and Matthew-Luke Jesus denies that a sign would be given. The Jews, however, both before and during Jesus' time, were accustomed to signs, and to looking for signs, and they interpreted the signs as illuminating, for those who could read them aright, an activity of God taking place or about to take place. When you see *this,* you will know *that.* Implied here was a one-to-one correspondence between the *sign* and the *action of God* to which it pointed. But the refusal of Jesus to give any sign at all implied that the "dominion of God" was *not* to be interpreted as a sign, but was a real symbol. Therefore its meaning could not be exhausted by any single, literal occurrence. For Jesus the "dominion of God" did not bear a one-to-one relationship to any single circumstance or event.

If it is correct that when Jesus spoke of the dominion of God he was not pointing to any particular historical happening, then our hermeneutical task is not to look for such a happening in history — for any signs of the end, or for the date or dates when the dominion of God will arrive. If, however, when Jesus referred to the dominion of God he was using a true symbol, then our hermeneutical task is to look for the many ways in which the experience of God as Sovereign may be visible in the lives of human beings.

The important question to be answered in order to interpret the Gospels is whether in Jesus' proclamation the "dominion of God" refers to a single, identifiable event, which every person would experience at exactly the same time, or whether the term refers to the coming of God in ways that can never be exhausted in or by any one event, but which every person may experience in her or his own time, each in her or his own way. Then it would be fruitless to speculate about what is the particular meaning of "dominion of God," or about when, where, or how it will be manifested.

If "dominion of God" is a true symbol, it will not bear a one-to-one relationship to any one event or circumstance. It will evoke a response or cluster of responses in those who read it or hear it preached—either an individual or a community—and those responses can only be talked about in metaphors and images.

Dominion of God
in the Gospels

It was shown in the last century that in Jewish literature God is often spoken of as "King," and that God's "kingdom" always means God's "rule" or "reign," not God's "realm." In Jewish literature "kingdom" of God never refers to a *place* where God rules, but always refers to the ruling activity itself. (See the discussion in chapter 4 of Psalm 145:10–13.)

The word "kingdom" in Psalm 145 always means "rule" or "reign," and never means "realm" or refers to any *place*. It is used in parallel with "power" and "mighty deeds." This is a typical example of the connotation of "kingdom" in Jewish literature. But does "kingdom" or "dominion" in Jesus' proclamation carry the same connotation or meaning as it apparently always does in Jewish literature? Or did Jesus use the expression "dominion of God" in a non-Jewish, astoundingly novel way, a way that made a lasting impression on Jesus' followers?

In the Gospels Jesus speaks of "entering" the dominion of God. Note such passages as Matt. 5:20: "For I tell you, unless your righteousness exceeds that of the scribes and Pharisees, you will never *enter* the dominion of heaven." (It has been shown that Matthew's usual expression "dominion of heaven" is not different in meaning from Mark's and Luke's consistent reference to the "dominion of God." "Heaven" is a typically Jewish circumlocution for "God.") Or, in Matt. 18:3: "Truly I tell you, unless you change and become like children, you will never *enter* the dominion of heaven." In Mark 9:47 Jesus says: "And if your eye causes you to stumble, tear it out; it is better for you to *enter* the dominion of God with one eye than to have two eyes and be thrown into hell." And in Mark 10:23 Jesus says: "How hard it will be for those who have wealth to *enter* the dominion of God!"

One "enters" the dominion of God as one "enters" into (eternal) life, or as one "enters" into a place. In Matt. 19:17 Jesus says, "If you wish to *enter* into life, keep the commandments." In Mark 9:43 Jesus says, "If your hand causes you to stumble, cut it off; it is better for you to *enter life* maimed than to have two hands and to go to hell, to the unquenchable fire"; but in Mark 9:47 Jesus says "it is better for you to *enter the dominion of God* with one eye than to have two eyes and to be thrown into hell." If Mark 9:47 is compared with Mark 9:43 we note that "entering the dominion of God" and "entering into life" are apparently synonymous terms. To enter the dominion of God *is* to enter into life.

The image that comes to mind when Jesus talks about the dominion of God, which one "enters," is the image of a place, or area, or sphere, or the image of life—life fulfilled. One does not "enter" into a *rule,* except in a derived sense, as the place where someone rules. One does, however, enter into a realm, or dominion, or kingdom. Apparently in Jewish literature there are no references to "entering" the dominion of God. Using the verb "to enter" with "dominion of God" seems to have been unique to Jesus.

Furthermore, Jesus speaks of persons or things as being "in" the dominion of God. In Matt. 5:19, just before Jesus talks about "entering the dominion of heaven" in Matt. 5:20, Jesus speaks twice of those who are "in" the dominion of heaven. Similarly Jesus refers to being "in" the dominion of heaven in Matt. 8:11 and 11:11. I have been told that in the Old Testament only in 1 Chron. 17:14, and in the Targum on that verse, does the expression "*in* the dominion" occur.

Jesus also speaks of the dominion of God as "coming." In the prayer taught by Jesus to the disciples, recorded by Matthew and Luke, we read the petition "May your dominion *come*" (Matt. 6:10 = Luke 11:2, author's translation). Note also Matt. 10:7; Matt. 12:28 = Luke 11:20; Matt. 16:28 = Mark 9:1, and so on. But Jesus does not speak in the typical Jewish way of the dominion as "appearing" or as being "revealed." Why is that?

In Jewish literature it is expected that God's "kingdom" or "dominion" will be established by the manifestation of the great power of God as "King," which will be revealed. Beginning with Old Testament literature, that expectation is widely shared in Judaism. How often, in Second Isaiah alone, do we read such passages as "the Sovereign God comes with might, and rules with a mighty arm" (Isa. 40:10)[5]; or "God delivers up nations to him (Cyrus), and tramples monarchs under foot" (Isa. 41:2b, author's translation); or "Thus says God to God's anointed, to Cyrus, whose right hand I have grasped to subdue nations before him and strip monarchs of their robes, to open doors before him—and the gates shall not be closed: I will go before you and level the mountains, I will break in pieces the doors of bronze and cut through the bars of iron . . ." (Isa. 45:1–2, author's translation). Manifestations of God's rule are frequently understood as manifestations of a mighty God who acts in the world with unmatched power—decisively and definitively.

If the Gospels make anything clear about Jesus, however, it is that Jesus had no such understanding of either the God he worshiped, or of his own life in relation to God; neither did Jesus think of the manifestation of God's dominion in a typically Jewish way. In Mark 10:35ff. Jesus tells James and John, who ask him for special favors, that rather than receiving special favors, they will suffer; and he asks them whether they are "able to drink the cup that (he drinks), or to be baptized with the baptism with which (he) is baptized"—clear references to Jesus' suffering and death. Recall Jesus' speaking of the "cup" in reference to his death in the prayer recorded later in all three synoptic Gospels: "Abba, Father-Mother, . . . remove this *cup* from me" (Mark 14:36 and parallels, Inclusive Version). And to shed light on the meaning of the reference to the disciples' ability to be "baptized" with Jesus' "baptism," note what Jesus says in Luke: "I have a baptism to be baptized with; and how I am constrained [or 'afflicted' or 'distressed'] until it is accomplished!" (Luke 12:50). The reference to the "baptism" Jesus is yet to face is undoubtedly an allusion to his death. So the question Jesus puts to the disciples in Mark 10:38 becomes a question about their ability to participate in any way in Jesus' "baptism."

Returning to Mark 10:35ff: After the disciples assure Jesus that indeed they *are* able to drink Jesus' cup and be baptized with Jesus' baptism, clearly not understanding Jesus' question, Jesus tells them that they *will* indeed drink Jesus' cup and be baptized with Jesus' baptism (Mark 10:39). Then follows Jesus' very stern warning to the disciples against their own manifestations of power. Among the Gentiles, Jesus says, the great people are those who act like tyrants, who exert power over others, and to this day our history books still talk mostly about such people. But to the disciples Jesus says that "whoever wishes to become great among you must minister to you, and whoever wishes to be first among you will be servant of all," just as Jesus also "came not to be served but to serve, and to give up life as a ransom for many" (Mark 10:42–45, Inclusive Version). Greatness is not to be found or measured in the exertion of might, but in the manifestation of aid, support, and care for others.

Where did Jesus get such a notion about greatness? Not from passages like the ones we have quoted from Second Isaiah, but from very different Old Testament passages, including certainly Second Isaiah's so-called "Servant Songs." Jesus got his clues not from such words as "For the nation and kingdom that will not serve you shall perish" (Isa. 60:12a), but from such words as "Comfort, O comfort my people, says your God. Speak tenderly to Jerusalem . . ." (Isa. 40:1–2a); or "Surely this one has borne our griefs and carried our sorrows; yet we esteemed the servant stricken, smitten by God, and afflicted. But this servant was wounded for our transgressions, was bruised for our iniquities, bore the chastisement that made us whole and the stripes by which we are healed" (Isa. 53:4–5).[6] In Judaism the dominion of God typically vindicates the righteous with great power, and by the same power the unrighteous are put down; but Jesus, like the author of the Servant Songs, does not speak about putting down the unrighteous, but goes out to the unrighteous, and the sick, the poor, and the dispossessed.

Jesus Christ

Many scholars think that when Jesus used the word "coming" in speaking about the dominion of God, Jesus was thinking of the "rule" or "reign" of God, the exertion of God's power to be manifested at the end of history. This is also a view that is widely shared in the church—that the "kingdom of God" is going to be revealed when God, in God's omnipotence, establishes it, once and for all, for everybody who deserves to enter it. But would Jesus have used the verb "enter" when referring to a "rule" or "manifestation of power"? Perhaps Jesus' understanding of the dominion of God had nothing to do with the manifestation of God's great power, as the texts just quoted would indicate, but centered on a "space" or "place of grace" which was already "coming" into the world, which God was "sending" into the world in Jesus' work and preaching.

When Jesus spoke of the dominion of God he would not have been talking about the beginning of God's rule in history, or the exercise of God's power in a new and decisive way in history. Jesus would have believed, along with all Jews, that God was always acting in history. What is new in Jesus' preaching is not belief in the coming all-powerful rule of God. What is new in Jesus' preaching is his reference to a new possibility of existence, to a new state of affairs that is "coming" now into the world, to change the conditions of the lives of people who are open to it. In Jesus' preaching the "coming" of the dominion of God has to do with an event impinging on the daily life of a man or woman, with a restorative power being exercised by Jesus—not with God's punishment or salvation, but with Jesus' healing and blessing of individuals and of the community around Jesus.

Along with the verb "coming," Jesus speaks of "inheriting" the dominion of God (Matt. 25:34), just as he speaks of "inheriting" eternal life (Matt. 19:29; Mark 10:17 = Luke 18:18; Luke 10:25). Jesus' emphasis seems to have been more on the salvation of humanity than on the manifestation of the power of God. Of course the former depends on the latter for its existence: God's activity is the precondition of salvation, and the "dominion" of God presupposes the "rule" of God. But "rule" of God is usually interpreted as meaning "overruling power" of God, whereas Jesus was not speaking about the overruling power of God, but about the restorative power of salvation—and not of the "righteous," but of the "sick." It appears, in short, that Jesus' emphasis was more on the *provision* than it was on the *Provider*.[7]

Jesus likened the dominion of God to a "banquet" (Matt. 22:2–14). In Luke 14:15 Jesus says, "Blessed is anyone who will eat bread in the dominion of God," and then Luke records the parable of the great dinner, which is similar to Matthew's parable of the banquet (Luke 14:15–24). In Luke Jesus also says: "When you give a banquet, invite the poor, the crippled, the lame, and the blind" (Luke 14:13)—all those to whom Jesus goes and heals in his ministry, not the righteous.

According to Matt. 12:25ff. and parallels, Jesus also likened the dominion of God to a "room" or "city" or "house," that is, to a sphere, space, or place of grace. In Matt. 12:25 Jesus says, "Every dominion [kingdom] divided against itself is laid waste, and no city or house divided against itself will stand." In this verse "dominion" or "kingdom" has the same kind of spatial meaning as "city" or "house." And "dominion" or "kingdom" in v. 26 has the same meaning as it does in v. 25; that is, it has a spatial reference: "If Satan casts out Satan, Satan is divided against Satan; how then will Satan's dominion [kingdom] stand?" (Matt. 12:26, author's translation). Satan's "kingdom" or "dominion" is a place, and Satan's "kingdom" does not refer to the "rule" of Satan, but to the place where Satan rules. So when we come to v. 28 where Jesus says, "If it is by the Spirit of God ["finger of God" in Luke] that I cast out demons, then the dominion of God has come upon you," "dominion of God" in all probability does not refer to the "rule" of God here either, but it describes a space or a place of living that has "come to you."

When in that verse Jesus speaks of the dominion of God as coming "upon" people, the meaning of "upon" must be that God's dominion, or place of grace, is encountering people in their historical existence. If Jesus, by the "Spirit" or "finger" of God, casts out demons (Matt. 12:28), then the place where God's dominion is to be met is a historical reality. According to the pericope of Matt. 12:22–29, the proof of the dominion's having arrived is Jesus' deliverance of the person who was possessed with a demon (see v. 22) from the power of Satan. To sum up, in Jesus' view the dominion of God is not a series of events accomplished by the powerful rule of God, but is a state of affairs proclaimed in Jesus' preaching. It is the realm, or space, or place of grace where healing and blessing are given and received. And *what* is given and received is *what is needed.* The dominion of God is not to be found simply in exorcisms, which in no way constitute the meaning of the dominion of God. But where there is possession by a demon, in that situation an exorcism is the manifestation of the presence and activity—or dominion—of God.

In the last chapter we observed that a symbol works by evoking images, and that the images evoked will always depend on the individual who hears or otherwise confronts the symbol. To a person possessed by a demon, the symbol of the dominion of God will evoke the image of an exorcism, of the demon's being expelled; but no one who is not possessed will think of exorcism in connection with the dominion of God. To a woman who was hemorrhaging, however, the dominion of God symbolized the cessation of her bleeding, which was, in fact, accomplished (cf. Mark 5:25–34 and parallels); and to a Roman centurion whose servant was "lying home paralyzed, in terrible distress," the presence of the dominion of God meant the healing of the servant (Matt. 8:5–13 = Luke 7:1–10). To a leper the dominion of God evoked the image of cleansing, and the presence of the dominion of God established that cleansing (Mark 1:40–44 and parallels); and to Jairus the symbol of the dominion of God evoked the image of the raising to life of his daughter, which was, in fact, accomplished by the dominion's presence (Mark 5:22–24, 35–42 and parallels). In each case the symbol "dominion of God" evoked what was needed by the individual, and in the presence of the "dominion of God," which was coming into the world, the image became historical reality, a present place of grace.

I think it is clear that in Jesus' time and in the time when the Gospels were written the expression "dominion of God" was extremely evocative and affective. Its impact on the disciples must have been extraordinary and unforgettable—hence the many references in the Gospels to Jesus' expression of this symbol, and to Jesus' activity on its behalf.

Nothing has been said here about another aspect of Jesus' preaching of the dominion of God—namely, its consummation in God's own time. It is clear from the Gospels that Jesus announced not only the presence of God's dominion in Jesus' life and work, but that Jesus also looked forward to the time when the dominion of God—the place of grace—would be fulfilled and would fill all. Space, however, does not permit discussion of this future aspect of Jesus' preaching which, in any case, is far more commonly assented to than the emphasis made here.

[10]

Signs in Mark
of the Dominion of God

Let us look now at two narratives in Mark that illustrate the presence of the dominion of God in Jesus' activity.

1. An exorcism. The first exorcism Mark records is placed just after the call of the first disciples. It is told very succinctly in Mark 1:21–26. One sabbath, when Jesus was teaching in the synagogue of Capernaum, there was a person in the synagogue "with (or *in*) an unclean spirit" (v. 23). The symptoms of the possessed person have been thought to indicate hysteria, having mental symptoms of delirium (stupor), convulsions, and double or multiple personality. Whether it was the person, or the unclean spirit who "cried out" is not certain, but probably it was the unclean spirit, for it refers to itself in the plural in v. 24: "What have you to do with *us*?" And later, "Have you come to destroy *us*?" And immediately this unclean spirit identifies Jesus by name: "Jesus of Nazareth," and further: "I (shifting to the singular pronoun) know who you are, the Holy One of God."

This demon's identification of Jesus by name, followed immediately by a *messianic* identification of Jesus, is enormously significant. It indicates the great fear on the part of the demon that Jesus will dislodge it. (I refer to the demon by the neuter pronoun [it], rather than by the masculine pronoun [he], not because I believe that demons have no gender, or no personal qualities, but because I do not know which gender to attribute to this demon, and because in normal English usage a demon is usually, if not always, an "it.")

Signs in Mark of the Dominion of God

The important point here, however, is not the gender of demons, but the fact of the demon's identification of Jesus, not by name only, but also by title. As I have said, this identification indicates not simply that the demon has supernatural knowledge, but also that the demon is using the best tool available to it to disarm Jesus of his power to do it any harm. The identification of Jesus as the "Holy One of God" is not for the purpose of complimenting Jesus, but grows out of the demon's panic that the Messiah (the Holy One of God), whom it now confronts, will attack it and render it impotent. The demon wants to stay where it is, and an exorcist is always its enemy. The "possessed" person is threatened. The demon is terrified. It clings to its dwelling and resists every effort to drive it out.

The demon's "crying out" to Jesus that Jesus is the "Holy One of God"—correctly identifying Jesus as Messiah—assumes the ancient belief that to know the name of a person is to possess the person's real identity, and therefore to have power over the person. This is not nonsense. It is something all human beings know deep down to be true. To identify, one must have the name; and to have the name is to have power over. One knows this even in the most superficial sense.

If there is no name, there is no identity. If you do not know the name of a person, you do not know the person except from a distance, only as an example of a genus and species to whom you are related in an impersonal way. But if you know a person's name, you are at least beginning to know who the person is, what some of the characteristics of the person are. Knowing the name means having a degree of knowledge; and to know a person is to know the name. The name and the person are the same. If I say, "Mary was there," I mean that the person, Mary, was there, and not just the name.

In the same way, to love God's *name* is to love *God*. In speaking to God the psalmist says, "Spread your protection over them, so that those who love your name may exult you" (Ps. 5:11). And to call on God's *name* is to call on *God*. Psalm 105:1 says, "O give thanks to God, call on God's *name,* make known God's deeds among the peoples" (Inclusive Version). And in 2 Samuel 22:50

we read, "For I will extol you, O God, among the nations, and sing praises to your *name*." To sing praises to the *name* of God is to sing praises to *God*. So also, to know the name of God is to know God.

In connection with people, the name by which you call another person designates the character and the degree of your knowledge of the person. (It is, of course, not different with God. God gave Israel God's intimate name, which only Israel knew, and it became too holy even to pronounce.) But in connection with people, if I say "Mister Jones" I do not know the person as well as one who calls him "Bob." And if Bob is my husband or intimate partner, and I call him by some intimate and private name, then by use of that name, I identify and "name" my special relationship. The name by which you call another indicates the relationship you have with the other, and an intimate name indicates intimacy.

In most European languages there are two pronouns that may be used in addressing other people—the pronoun commonly used when speaking to another, and the pronoun used only when speaking to another with whom one is very intimate—a child, a spouse, a close relative, a very close friend. The intimate pronoun identifies the relationship.

When my family and I were living in Fenin, a very small town in French-speaking Switzerland outside of Neuchâtel, as the months went by we grew ever closer to the pastor of the villages in the valley in which we lived. The pastor was exceedingly kind to us and took care of us often in times of need. He looked after us. The pastor and his wife would have us all over for Sunday dinner, and we became very fond of them both. But he was always "Monsieur," and she was always "Madame," and my wife and I were also "Madame" and "Monsieur" to them. When we left their valley to drive to what was then West Berlin, where I was to teach in the Kirchliche Hochschule, we said our last "Au revoir" to Monsieur and Madame Favre. Later we corresponded with each other, and we continued to address each other always in the same way, as "Monsieur" and "Madame."

Some years after we left Switzerland, when I was attending a conference at Oxford University, I planned to go down to southern France to visit the Favres in their beautiful home in the wine country to which they had retired. M. Favre was not well, but he and his wife greeted me at the train station warmly and drove me out to their home in the countryside. That night they took me out to dinner in a little restaurant, down a narrow street, where the owner of the restaurant greeted them with great affection; and some time during the dinner Monsieur Favre addressed me for the first time as "tu" rather than "vous"—the intimate French pronoun, and called me "Burton." I, of course, responded in the same way. He was older than I, and he was the one to initiate use of the intimate name.

That simple change in pronouns altered our relationship rather dramatically. By the use of the intimate pronoun and the first name I had been invited to "come into" their space, to share life with Fernand and Madeleine in a place new for all of us.

But with a new, more intimate relationship comes also a new vulnerability. When another is invited in to share one's life more intimately, one lets down barriers and becomes more subject to the other. As one's self-disclosure is increased, the possibility of the new knowledge being used against one is correspondingly greater. So it is that one exposes oneself to another only after one has arrived at a situation of trust.

Now back to the demon who, in exposing Jesus' true identity as Messiah, tried to establish power over Jesus: "I know who you are, the Holy One of God." A battle between Jesus and the demon had begun, and the battle had cosmic implications: it was the battle between the Messiah and the power of evil manifested in a possessed person. Jesus was identified by supernatural demonic powers as the Messiah, but he was not so identified by the Jews in the synagogue in Capernaum. The demon tried to unmask Jesus before the crowd, and thus gain power over him. But Jesus rebuked the demon, commanding the demon to be silent and come out. And the unclean spirit, convulsing the person and calling out with a great voice, came out.

There can be little doubt that Jesus did exorcise demons—the testimony to such exorcisms is simply too widespread to deny. And after Jesus' death, in the early church as well, exorcisms "in the name of Jesus" took place. In the early 200s the church theologian Origen wrote that Celsus, who said that demons should be worshiped because they were powerful and could bring all kinds of trouble if they were not, had "never witnessed the efficacy of those words, 'in the name of Jesus,' when uttered by the truly faithful, to deliver not a few from demons and demoniacal possessions and other plagues."[1]

In our own time exorcisms "in the name of Jesus" are still being practiced. The late Archbishop Philip Carrington of Quebec told me once that in his homeland, New Zealand, he had often witnessed such exorcisms "in the name of Jesus." A priest would address a demon who had "possessed" a person with the powerful words, "In the name of Jesus, come out!" and the person typically would exhale a powerful breath, and bystanders would say, "The demon has gone." If a possessed man exhaled twice, it would be said, "He had two demons." If "possession" is the diagnosis, exorcism is the cure; exorcism presupposes possession.

One sabbath, in the synagogue in Capernaum, Jesus exorcised a person who had an unclean spirit. And Jesus said, "If I by the Spirit of God cast out demons, then the dominion of God has come upon you" (author's translation of Matt. 12:28; cf. Luke 11:20). That exorcism was a manifestation of the presence of the dominion of God, and it was accomplished by the Messiah, Jesus. Jesus' presence and activity unveiled the merciful healing power of God.

2. A healing. Later in his Gospel Mark records a quite different story of a woman who had an incurable disease and had been hemorrhaging for twelve years (Mark 5:25–34). She was poor, having spent everything she had on physicians, and her suffering was, in fact, getting worse. Meanwhile Jesus had crossed the lake to where this woman was—perhaps Capernaum—and he was surrounded by a great crowd of people. The woman had heard about Jesus, and worked her way through the crowd until she got to where he was. She believed if she could just touch his clothes, she would be "saved," as Mark says (Mark 5:28); she would be made whole again.

Signs in Mark of the Dominion of God

Because of her hemorrhaging this woman was, according to Jewish law, ceremoniously "unclean." And according to Leviticus 15:25ff., not only was she unclean, but anyone who even touched her, or her bed, or her chair would also be unclean. Because this woman was "unclean" and "in her impurity," she was completely estranged from her entire community, unable to touch or to be touched.

The fact is that according to Hebrew law *every* woman, when going through her *natural* life cycle—not sick, not infected, not abnormal in any way—every woman was "in her impurity" every month of the year by virtue of her menstruation (Lev. 15:19ff.). Every woman, in her natural state, was ceremonially unclean every month: "When a woman has a discharge of blood *that is her regular discharge from her body,* she shall be in her impurity for seven days" (Lev. 15:19). One should try to imagine what that means!

A man has no corresponding *natural* periods of "impurity"; he is unclean only when he has "an emission of semen," or "a discharge from his member" (Lev. 15:2). But women suffered for the "impurity" and "uncleanness" which was decreed for them by their very biological nature.

The woman described in Mark's story had been hemorrhaging for twelve years. This is the situation referred to in Lev. 15:25ff.: "a discharge of blood for many days, not at the time of her impurity." Leviticus says that "all the days of [such] a discharge she shall continue in uncleanness; as in the days of her impurity, she shall be unclean." So this woman, as portrayed in Mark, presumably had not been touched for twelve years, nor had she touched anyone.

It is very interesting to note that commentaries on the passage in Leviticus 15 raise no questions about the justice or injustice of such laws regarding men and women. They were written by men who were not particularly sensitive to the extraordinary punishment meted out to all women because they are women. One commentator notes that because menstruation was a "regular" case of uncleanness, it needed no special cleansing ceremony or sacrificial procedure—the woman was simply "impure" for seven days, and there was nothing to be done about it. He admits that menstruation is "regular" (or "natural"), but he does not draw any conclusions about the justice or injustice of considering the whole of the female sex "unclean" repeatedly year after year during their natural life cycles.[2]

Another commentator on Leviticus 15 says that v. 25 (which speaks about a woman who "has a discharge of blood for many days, not at the time of her impurity") "insists on there being no intercourse at all [as] the woman is *unwell* [sic!]." He continues: "So again we meet with suggestions about tenderness, affection and self-control in the married state, and the need by the male to respect the rhythmical cycle of a woman's sexual being."[3] But in fact Lev. 15:25 does not talk about the "rhythmical cycle of a woman's sexual being," but it talks about a woman with an *abnormal* discharge of blood. In any case, we have here a good example of the "put-the-lady-on-the-pedestal" syndrome, no matter what suffering or injustice it may cause her.

To return to Mark's story: This woman had had a flow of blood for twelve years—for twelve years she had been in a state of "uncleanness," and had not touched or been touched. She came up to Jesus and *touched* his outer garment. At that moment, according to Hebrew law, *Jesus* became ritually unclean (cf. Lev. 15:19b). This woman, unnamed, has touched another, Jesus—and she is *healed.* Rather than her making Jesus unclean, Jesus makes her well. Wholeness characterizes the dominion of God, which becomes present in the person of Jesus. And God's dominion is not contaminated by someone "unclean"; on the contrary, God's dominion *includes,* and takes in, and transforms, and heals, and makes whole a person whom the community judges to be unclean, impure, and contaminating.

The perspective of life in God's dominion is not a human perspective. In God's dominion the first are last, and the last are first, and human constructs are demolished. Mark's story also indicates the connection between the person of Jesus and the dominion of God. The presence of God's dominion is manifested in the presence of the person of Jesus, in whose presence there is healing never before possible in our world. And at the end of the narrative Jesus calls the woman "Daughter," thereby reassuring her of her acceptance. "Daughters" as well as "sons" participate in the dominion of God. Jesus' final word is, "Your *faith* has *saved* [Mark's word] you." That statement undercuts a too-miraculous interpretation of the healing. But the healing is described as her "salvation," made possible by her faith in Jesus.

This story is told from the woman's point of view. She seeks out Jesus; Jesus does not seek her. She touches Jesus and is healed; Jesus does not "heal" her. Jesus asks who touched him—thus highlighting the incident, calling attention to it. And the woman is saved by *her* faith, her coming to Jesus in the belief that Jesus could save her.

If Jesus' presence by the Spirit of God brings salvation, then the dominion of God has come upon you.

[11]

The Dominion
of God Today

In our day, by virtue of centuries of repetition, the symbol "dominion of God" appears to have largely lost its evocative power.
When mentioned today it is apt to produce yawns, or a polite tol-
erance. The symbol usually fails to create life-saving images, and
its life-saving potential in the world goes unrecognized. Rather,
the symbol is usually intended and heard as a nonevocative sign,
pointing to an earth-shattering act of God some time in the future—usually in the far distant future, with very little relevance for
the daily lives of believers. The question remains for the church today: How can the symbol regain its power?

It has been true from the earliest days of the church that faithful preaching is what communicates the heart of the gospel, and
somewhere near that heart lies the symbol "dominion of God."
Paul wrote to the Romans that "everyone who calls on the name of
the Lord shall be saved." Then he asks: "But how are they to call
on one in whom they have not believed? And how are they to believe in one of whom they have never heard? *And how are they to
hear without someone to preach*? And how are they to preach unless they are sent?" (Rom. 10:14–15a, Inclusive Version). Paul is
very clear here, and I have no idea how anything but preaching and
other witnessing to the gospel can restore the power of the symbol
"dominion of God." The trick, of course, is in fashioning preaching, and fashioning all one's witness, so that hearers or readers will
once again be enabled to respond to the symbolic intention of the
expression "dominion of God," and will be moved to be open to
experience it. The question involves how to see, as well as how to

tell. It pertains to lenses and feelings and imagination and faith. Only God is able to effect a miracle, but Jesus and Jesus' disciples are still a medium through which God works. A discussion of how preaching can affect faith would demand a book-length treatise; and discussions of many kinds are required if the gospel is once again to evoke the transformation of human life.

One must attune oneself to looking for the hand of God in daily life, to looking for the presence of Jesus, or of the Spirit, or of the power of the Creator, or of the Source of all being. God appointed Jeremiah "to pluck up and to pull down, to destroy and to overthrow, to build and to plant" (Jer. 1:10). We must look for the hand of God and try to discern how or in what ways God is acting in the affairs of the nations, "to pluck up or to pull down," and how and in what ways God is acting in the affairs of individual lives.

At the very end of the Gospel of Matthew, Jesus' final words to the disciples—who had met Jesus on a mountain in Galilee, and had just worshiped Jesus—were, "Remember, I am with you always, to the end of the age" (Matt. 28:20b). The question is: Does one believe that also today Jesus is "with" Jesus' followers? Does one take Jesus' promise to heart? Does one look for the presence of Jesus in the church, in the community, in one's own life, and in the lives of others? Does one thank Jesus for blessings? Does one thank God? Is one sensitive to Jesus' presence, searching for what Jesus is doing or saying? What lens does one look through? Out of what construct does one live one's life?

To appropriate the power of Jesus' symbol "dominion of God," one must assume the presence of the Jesus who preached it. It would be futile to look for the "dominion of God" announced by Jesus if one did not believe in the one whose symbol it was and is. It was the historical person Jesus who was the symbol of the "dominion of God," and who gave definition in concrete words and acts to the meaning of the symbol. One must follow Jesus, and must carefully observe Jesus, in order to begin to understand and to expect manifestations of the dominion preached by Jesus who made it present. Jesus has always been and still remains the heart of the gospel; regardless of where one reads in the New

Testament—the Gospels, Paul's letters, or anywhere else—that statement always holds.

If one reads Paul, one ponders the significance of the life and death and continuing presence in the church of that same historical person, Jesus, through whom "by faith" one is "made righteous" before God. And if one reads the Gospels, one also is required to listen to the witness of the church, as represented in four different communities, as to who Jesus was. The great question in the church today centers on the issue of the significance of the varieties of the witnesses to Jesus that one finds in the Gospels, and on decisions one makes about which witnesses speak the most clearly. To talk about the "real" Jesus, the Jesus who lies behind all historical reconstructions, one has to arrange the multiple witnesses found in the four Gospels in a descending order of importance. But still more significant than the distinctions one makes in judging the degree of authenticity of various verses in the Gospels is the issue of how much meaning such an arrangement of Gospel material has for the life and faith of the believer.

The church did not canonize *sayings* of Jesus, just as it did not canonize *manuscripts* of the Gospels. The church canonized four *books* of the New Testament as Gospels—Matthew, Mark, Luke, and John. The aphorisms spoken by Jesus are no *more* "gospel" than Jesus' sayings in the Sermon on the Mount, or Jesus' parables, or the history of Jesus depicted in the Gospels. All are gospel. This means that the distinctions between the various sayings of Jesus in the Gospels—distinctions made by various New Testament scholars—have no *ultimate* significance for the *church*. They have no ultimate significance for preaching in the church; they have no ultimate significance for the piety of believers in the church.

When, as a very young man many years ago, I began the serious study of the New Testament, I was quite sure that given time I would master it all; I would be able to ascertain with some assurance the dimensions and the character and the intention of the "real" Jesus. I learned after some time, however, that one does not "master" the New Testament. One *loves* the New Testament more and more, but one does not "master" it. Furthermore, one's basic

The Dominion of God Today

commitments in faith are not fundamentally altered either by one's ever-changing historical-critical judgments, or by the judgments of others. That is the way it must always be. The church canonized the whole of the four Gospels, and not just the verses deemed "authentic" by the most recent investigations of any particular scholar or group of scholars.

Having said that, however, it is important to add that one's critical study of the Gospels will always affect the way one understands them. I can illustrate this by the following poem, "Exodus," written by Marge Piercy:

> Out of cattle pen tenement
> where the will to live fades out
> like a forty watt bulb in the hallway's crotch;
> out of streets rampant with proud metal
> where men are mice at work
> and slavering dogs afterward;
> out of beds where women offer up
> their only part prized whose name
> is an insult and means woman here;
> where anxiety yellows the air;
> where greed paints over every window;
> where defeat private as a worm
> gnaws every belly,
> we begin our slow halting exodus.
> Egypt, you formed me from your clay.
> I am a doll baked in your factory ovens,
> yet I have risen and walked.
>
> Like the Golem I am makeshift, lumbering.
> I rattle and wheeze and my parts
> are cannibalized T-birds and sewing machines,
> mixers and wheelchairs, hair dryers.
> My skin is the papier-mâché of newspapers
> cured with the tears of children
> pregnant with hunger. My heart
> is the stolen engine of an F-111.

Jesus Christ

My ligaments are knitting needles, hangers
recovered from the bodies of
self-aborted women. My teeth are military
headstones. I am the Golem.
Many breathed rage and hope into my
lungs, their roar
is my voice, their dreams
burning are my fuel.
They say nothing but a desert stretches
beyond, where the skulls of visionaries
are scoured by ants.

We have entered our Thirty Years' War
for a green place called the Country
of the Living. For two generations
we will be walking to a land we must build,
ourselves the bricks, the boards, the bridges,
in every face the map,
in every hand the highway.
We go clanking, stumbling forward, lurching.
Children born in that country
will play in the wreckage of our fears.[1]

If this poem were to be dug up a thousand years from now, what
would the reader make of it? If one knew nothing about the contents of the Bible, the references to the "exodus" and to "Egypt"
would not be grasped at all. And if one did know the Bible but did
not pick up the deeper meaning of the poem, one would still have
no idea why the references to the "exodus" and "Egypt" had been
included. Furthermore, a thousand years from now a reader would
have to wonder what in the world a "T-bird" was, or an "F one hundred and eleven," as it would probably be read, or what "sewing
machines" and "hair dryers" used to be. Why had they been necessary? What did they accomplish, and what kind of culture would
require them? Clarification of all these terms would depend entirely on the investigations of historical critics. A commentary on
the poem would help the reader understand, and would illuminate

the poem immensely. In fact, without the work of such a critic the poem would largely remain a riddle.

Historical criticism of the Bible serves exactly the function of illuminating obscurities of language and historical references, thus shedding light on its meaning. But historical criticism alone cannot illuminate the full meaning of a text, and other criticisms must come into play. Finally, a hermeneutics is required which, in turn, presupposes an understanding of the deeper message of the text that one has gained, other than from the text itself. There has to be a point of contact between the text one is reading and the life and experience of the person reading it. Let me illustrate with the poem quoted above.

After the historical critic has done her or his work, and has made it possible for the reader to grasp the intentions of the historical references and the meanings of difficult words and phrases in the poem, one would still not be enabled to grasp its full significance. Much more important than the meaning of specific terms and references would be a discussion of the deeper, underlying meaning of the poem, and that would depend on an analysis of the poem's cultural context as well as the poet's reaction to that context.

The poem quoted above is, of course, highly critical of modern technological society. It is even more critical of the role foisted on women in our culture, and of the characteristic images held of women. So in order to understand the poem a reader a thousand years hence would have to investigate the many ways in which women were oppressed in our society, often in very subtle ways. Then if one had no sympathy with that oppression, one would be put off by the poem's language, and would not grasp the significance of such images as "Egypt," the "exodus," and the "Golem." One cannot begin to understand these and many other images of the poem if one has no prior feeling for, or reaction to, the situation of women it is talking about. The poem is not comprehensible apart from a previous understanding of the specific cultural and social contexts it describes. The poem's images may elicit a profound response to the injustices of this present situation, and they depend for their power on a participation of the hearer or reader in the poet's experience. But there is always the possibility that the reader will not understand it at all, will not be able to identify with any of it, will not be moved, and will remain unchanged.

So it is with the Gospels, or with the reading of any scripture. The writing sheds light on what one knows otherwise and on other grounds. Life in Christ and the reading of the Gospels go hand in hand. Each informs the other. One knows Christ by reading the Gospels, and one understands the Gospels by knowing Christ.

[12]

Jesus and the Law

With regard to one's relation to the Jewish law, what were the implications of the presence of the dominion of God in Jesus and in Jesus' activity? Did Jesus believe that the law was not relevant in face of the reality of the coming dominion of God? Did Jesus believe that he and his disciples were subject to the law, and if so, how was obedience to the law related to the coming dominion of God? Did their obedience to the law hasten the dominion's coming? Or was their obedience to the law irrelevant to the coming of the dominion of God? What did the coming of God's dominion imply for the authority of the Torah, of God's law for Israel? Mark's narrative about the disciples plucking heads of grain on the sabbath (2:23–28) gives us some insight into these matters. But first, we should look at the Jewish understanding of the law in Jesus' time, even if very briefly.

In Jesus' time the scribes copied the law, interpreted it, and sought to obey it. The Pharisees, who were lay people and were the most influential group in Judaism, also rigorously attempted to keep the Torah throughout all of everyday life. In Neh. 10:30ff., written just before or just after 300 B.C.E., we find the beginning of the legalism that was to characterize Jewish life. Nehemiah says that "if people of the land bring in wares or any grain on the sabbath day to sell, we will not buy from them on the sabbath or on a holy day" (10:31). Here is an early law regarding how the sabbath law is to be obeyed and what the sabbath law forbids.

The Pharisees, who interpreted the law as obligatory in all of daily life, were a progressive group; that is, they kept altering the requirements of the law as their circumstances changed. They took the law with utter seriousness, and adapted it to new situations as they arose. And, of course, the inevitable happened: the number of laws kept increasing—laws pertaining not only to the sabbath, but also to ritual cleansings, to eating, to prayers, and so on. If the sabbath law was to be kept, it had to be kept in every area of life; if it were broken at even one point, one was guilty. Percentages of obedience do not count. Let us, then, look at one law, the sabbath law, and see how it was implemented.

The Decalogue (that is, the Ten Commandments) flatly prohibits work on the sabbath. Exodus 20:8ff. says, "Remember the sabbath day, and keep it holy. . . . you shall not do any work—you, your son or your daughter, your male or female slave, your livestock, or the alien resident in your towns." Very clear, but very imprecise. The question that must still be answered is, what is *work*? "You shall not do any work," it says, but exactly what constitutes work? If the law is to be kept, everything hinges on the answer to that question. For example, the question arose among the Jews, Does the sabbath law permit rescuing an animal that has fallen into a well on the sabbath? May one keep food hot on the fire on the sabbath? May one become engaged to be married on the sabbath— is engagement work? If the sabbath law is to be kept, answers to these and what would become hundreds of other similar questions had to be sought. Schools of interpretation of the law arose, and these interpretations became the ways according to which the laws of Torah might be obeyed.

It is very important for us to remember that the matter of obedience was of such magnitude among the Jews because the law of Moses was believed to have been given by *God*. With regard to other laws—family laws, civil laws—one has a certain freedom to obey or not to obey. If, for example, one came to a stop sign at a crossroad in the middle of an open plain, and one could not see a single car for miles around, one might take the liberty of exercising some discretion and deciding that, under the circumstances, one could disobey the law requiring one to stop, and one would likely suffer no pangs of conscience as a result. But if the law is understood to be given by God, then the question of whether or not discretion should play a role is not so easily settled. If the law is given by *God,* and is to be obeyed, is not one's duty obvious?

In our day civil laws are sometimes adopted to deal with the implementation of religious laws. For example, we have in this country the so-called Sunday "blue laws," which deal with questions of whether or not liquor stores are to be closed on Sunday. But what about booking agencies? In the recent past, and perhaps still in the present, the Virginia legislature's interpretation of the Sunday blue laws forbade one to sell a hat on the sabbath. However, one could sell a toy hat, such as a cowboy hat; and one could sell eggs if they were to be used raw, but not if they were to be cooked.

In the nation of Israel today there is often tension between parties regarding just how the sabbath law is to be implemented. Are movie and theater performances to be banned on the sabbath? Should football games be permitted? Should taxis run on the sabbath? So long as the sabbath law prohibiting work is in effect, there must be precise answers to the question of what constitutes work. In the Israel of Jesus' time it was the Pharisees who tried to answer the question of what constituted work, as well as all other questions related to the implementation of Torah. The Pharisees laid out concretely and minutely the ways in which the Torah was to be obeyed, and so long as the law remained in effect, one cannot blame them too quickly for legalism in laying out exactly how the laws were to be implemented. If the law was not completely binding, it was not in effect.

The way Judaism developed the means by which to obey the laws of Torah was to "hedge the laws about," as was said, by other, oral laws, which interpreted and applied the written laws of Torah. A network of such oral laws was developed in order to protect the laws of Torah. For example, the sabbath law became "hedged about" by thirty-nine different oral laws, stating that plowing, sowing, reaping, and so on were considered to be "work." In order to assure that the sabbath law would be kept, thirty-nine activities were stipulated as "work," so to engage in any one of them would be to break the law.

Of course, the next development would have to be the question of precisely what constituted *plowing,* or *sowing,* or *reaping.* If, for example, one dug out a line in the dirt by kicking it with one's foot, would one be guilty of plowing? If one picked a bunch of grapes as one was walking through the vineyards, would one be reaping? In order to protect the sabbath law, to keep it from being broken, answers to such questions as these would have to be established, and they were. It was determined, for instance, that sowing included planting trees and pruning them; plowing included not only harvesting grain but also picking grapes, cutting clusters of dates, and plucking olives and figs. And so there was developing in Jesus' time a large body of oral laws that, while secondary in importance to Torah itself, were the codified ways in which Torah was to be obeyed. These laws eventually came to specify in the minutest detail what Torah forbade and what it permitted.

Another development ensued. When life became so minutely regulated, and what one could and could not do so precisely defined, it followed that the degree to which one had obeyed or disobeyed the law, and therefore the degree to which one had obeyed or disobeyed God, could be calculated in a correspondingly precise manner. One could know exactly what laws one had disobeyed, or whether or not one was, in fact, "righteous." What one had done, one's behavior, would tell the whole story exactly, would *define* one's relationship to God.

And so there developed in some branches of Judaism a personal orientation primarily to the Torah, in relation to which one's standing with God could be determined. Torah became preeminent in the life of a faithful Jew. This development tended to place God in the position of becoming, in a secondary way, the one who ratified one's faithfulness to, or disobedience of, the Torah. God's freedom to judge was undermined, and God was reduced to being the rewarder of righteousness (which one had already achieved by one's performance under Torah), and the punisher of unrighteousness (which punishment one had already earned by disobedience of Torah). If it was in one's relation to Torah that one's destiny was determined, God did not have to be met day by day at all, but only at the end of life, when God would ratify the results of one's performance. God became the great "Rubber Stamper" in some areas of Jewish faith.

Different traditions of these oral laws developed over a long period of time, from the beginning of the second century B.C.E. to the conclusion of the second century of the Common Era, culminating in the Mishnah, which was inherited by Rabbi Judah the Patriarch and codified around 200 C.E. The Mishnah represented the movement of Israel to Judaism, and the triumph of Pharisaic Judaism in Israel. It also provided a link between Palestinian and non-Palestinian Judaism that proved to be strong enough to bind all Jews together.

Now let us return to Mark's story of Jesus and the disciples walking through the grainfields on the sabbath (2:23–28). Mark begins the story: "One sabbath he [Jesus] was going through the grainfields." Immediately the reader will wonder why it was that Jesus was going through the grainfields *on a sabbath.* The shock beginning immediately raises the question of whether the sabbath law will be broken. The answer to that question is given promptly: Jesus' disciples "began to pluck heads of grain." They were indeed breaking the sabbath law—they were "reaping." So some Pharisees quickly pointed out their breach of the law: "See here, why are they doing what is not lawful on the sabbath?" (2:24).

Jesus' answer to the Pharisees' judgment is extremely revealing of his attitude toward the law. He asked them a counterquestion: "Have you never read what David did when he and his companions were hungry and in need of food? He entered the house of God, when Abiathar was high priest, and ate the bread of the Presence, which it is not lawful for any but the priests to eat, and he gave some to his companions" (2:25–26). Jesus pointed out that the great King David, from whose house the Messiah would come, broke the sabbath law according to the way it was interpreted by many Jews of Jesus' time. David ate the "bread of the Presence," the twelve loaves which, according to Leviticus 24, are to be placed "in two rows, six in a row, on the table of pure gold. . . . Every sabbath day Aaron shall set them in order before the Sovereign regularly as a commitment of the people of Israel, as a covenant forever. *They shall be for Aaron and his descendants (the priests), who shall eat them in a holy place . . .* "

Jesus Christ

(Lev. 24:5–9, author's translation). But according to 1 Samuel 21, when David came to Nob, to the priest Ahimelech (not Abiathar, as Mark has it), he asked Ahimelech "for five loaves of bread, or whatever is here," for him and the "young men" who were then with him, and the priest answered David that he had no ordinary bread, but "only holy bread." The narrative goes on to say that the priest gave David the holy bread "for there was no bread there except the bread of the Presence" (1 Sam. 21:1–6). Jesus quoted scripture to demonstrate that the disciples' action was not different from that of David, who also broke the law in a circumstance that justified it. The point would seem to be that situations may arise that take precedence over the requirements of the law. David acted on this assumption, and Jesus' disciples did the same thing. If David was not guilty, neither were Jesus' disciples—this is Mark's interpretation of the incident.

An interesting sidelight is that both Matthew and Luke, who were following Mark very closely in this narrative, leave out Mark's historical error—that the incident with David occurred when Abiathar, rather than Ahimelech, was high priest (see Matt. 12:4 and Luke 6:4). Another difference in the way the story is told here is that Luke, alone of the three Synoptic Gospels, says that Jesus' disciples broke two of the oral laws—not only did they "pluck" ears of grain, but they also "rubbed them in their hands," breaking a second law against reaping or threshing.

After Jesus reminded the Pharisees who were present of what David had done "when he and his companions were hungry," Jesus added, "The sabbath was made for the human being, not the human being for the sabbath" (Mark 2:27, author's translation). Here Jesus very clearly rejected the Jews' interpretation of the meaning of the sabbath law, and therefore, from the point of view of the Pharisees, Jesus at the same time rejected the sabbath law itself. Jesus said that when the sabbath law "was made" (v. 27a) it was made "for the sake of" human beings, and not vice versa. The human being, humankind, was not created for the sake of the sabbath law—that is, in order that there be people to obey it—but the sabbath law was created for the sake of the human being. Human beings take precedence, in some sense, over the sabbath law.

Thus Jesus rejected the position that had become normative in Judaism—namely, that the Jews' *primary* obligation was to the law. What Jesus clearly implied was that Jesus' and the disciples' *primary* obligation was to *God* (though that is not explicitly stated), the One who comes near, whose dominion may be "entered" or appropriated.

Then Mark records a further word from Jesus. After "the sabbath was made for the human being, not the human being for the sabbath," Jesus added, "so that the Human One is sovereign even of the sabbath" (author's translation). The first statement about humankind's relation to the sabbath leads to the following consequence ("so that"): the Human One is sovereign even of the sabbath. It seems very likely that the latter clause was a deduction made by the church, recorded by the author of Mark and reiterated by Matthew and Luke. Matthew, in fact, greatly elaborated on that last clause. The deduction appears to be a comment from the church that expressed the conviction that Jesus, the Human One, was indeed sovereign over all things having to do with the disciples, including the sabbath law. The "Human One" was a title given Jesus by the church, having no inherent connotation but rather taking on significance according to its specific context.

As indicated, Matt. 12:1–8 greatly elaborated on the statement that the Human One was sovereign even of the sabbath. But first we should note that in the first verse Matthew added to his Marcan source the statement that the disciples *were hungry* when they plucked the heads of grain, drawing a parallel between the hunger of the disciples and the hunger of David and his companions (Matt. 12:3). And by the introduction of this single verb Matthew also indicated that there was a good reason why the disciples broke the sabbath—the same reason David had broken it—a reason not included in Mark. We may guess from this that the sabbath (our Saturday) was probably still kept by Matthew's church, though undoubtedly not as strictly as it was in many Jewish congregations.

Returning to Matthew's elaboration of Mark 2:27–28, both Matthew and Luke omit Jesus' statement in Mark that "the sabbath was made for the human being, and not the human being for the sabbath," but Matthew has put two of his own additional statements on Jesus' lips. The first is, "Have you not read in the law that on the sabbath the priests in the temple break the sabbath and yet are guiltless? I tell you something greater than the temple is here" (12:5–6). This statement reinforces the significance of Jesus' earlier word about David's breaking the law and remaining guiltless. For 1 Samuel 21 does not say that David broke the *sabbath* law, but that he broke a different law, one that forbids any but the priests to eat the bread of the Presence. But then Matthew has Jesus raise the question of whether his hearers have not read in the law that on the sabbath the priests in the temple break the *sabbath* and are still guiltless, thus creating a parallel to what the disciples have just done on the sabbath.

Similarly, Num. 28:9–10 records God's command to Moses that a burnt offering is to be made for every sabbath *on the sabbath day*. Matthew quotes that passage to show that even according to the law itself, the sabbath law may be broken in accordance with the will of God. And Matthew adds that "something greater than the sabbath is here" (12:6), arguing here from the smaller to the greater. What is meant by "something greater than the sabbath" is not altogether clear. Perhaps the Messiah is the "something greater"—there are, in fact, late manuscripts of Matthew that have Jesus say, "*Someone* greater than the temple is here." Still, one cannot be sure that Matthew was referring to Jesus; the "something greater" may well have been the community around Jesus. The comparison at any rate seems to be between the priests in the Temple and the disciples of Jesus. Matthew would then be making the point that Jesus' disciples are protected by the Messiah, that they are "greater" than the Temple, and that what they have done in the presence of the Messiah cannot be considered blameworthy.

In 12:7 Matthew quotes Hos. 6:6, "I desire mercy and not sacrifice." Jesus tells the accusers that if they had known what Hosea's text meant, they would not have condemned those who were guiltless—the disciples. Both priests and the Temple have been referred to in the two previous sections of the narrative, and this reference to "sacrifice" fits into that context. The point of the quotation from Hosea is that *mercy* is what God desires, and food for the hungry is merciful.

Matthew's insertion of 12:5–7 into the Marcan context highlights and gives a climactic emphasis to Jesus' culminating statement: "The Human One is sovereign of the sabbath." But Matthew has also made a small addition to Mark that heightens Jesus' statement; Matthew has added the word "for." All the preceding statements made by Jesus lead up to the concluding statement: "*For* the Human One is sovereign of the sabbath."

It is to be noted that in none of the Gospel accounts of this story has Jesus rejected the sabbath law. Jesus never says that the law is no longer binding. What Jesus says in all three accounts of the narrative is that the Messiah is sovereign *over* the law. The law remains in effect, and Jesus is its sovereign.

The narrative that follows the story of Jesus and the disciples in the grainfields brings into even greater clarity the point just made. It is the story of the person with the "withered hand" in Mark 3:1–6, and in the passages that are roughly parallel in Matt. 12:9–14 and Luke 6:6–11. Here again we have a story that takes place on the sabbath, this time in a synagogue. Only Matthew says that the incident took place in "*their* synagogue" (12:9). Thus Matthew distinguishes between his own Jewish-Christian synagogue (*our* synagogue) and the synagogue of the Jews (*their* synagogue). By making this distinction the Jewish author of Matthew relates his worshiping community directly to the Jewish historical person Jesus, but he distinguishes his Jewish-Christian community from the *other* Jewish community from which it had separated.

Now we will continue with Mark 3:1–6. Jesus entered a synagogue on the sabbath where there was a person with a "withered hand." The person was paralyzed, perhaps from birth, which would mean that the situation was in no sense an emergency. If a healing were to take place it could certainly wait until nightfall, when the sabbath would be over. Mark says that "they" watched Jesus. Who were "they"? Mark does not say, but the last reference to any people was to Pharisees in Mark 2:24, and Mark 3:6 speaks about "Pharisees" going out to conspire against Jesus. In any case, these people were lying in wait to see whether Jesus would break the sabbath, so that if he did, they could bring charges against him. The scene was set. They were watching, and Jesus acted.

Jesus said to the paralyzed person, "Step forward," "Come up to me." Obviously the person obeyed; and then Jesus asked those waiting for him to break the sabbath the following surprising and utterly baffling question: "Is it lawful to do good or to do harm on the sabbath, to save life or to *kill*?" The text says they were silent (Mark 3:4). You bet they were! What could they answer?

The scene describes people hoping to trap Jesus performing an act of mercy that would break the law. The fact that an act of mercy can break the law is itself of some interest. These people were "righteous" people, who kept the law. We have before us the irony of "good" people (with evil hearts) trying to ensnare a person who, from their point of view, would be evil if he broke the sabbath in a merciful act. Are these onlookers who themselves keep the law, and are hoping to catch Jesus in a misstep, "good"? And would Jesus be evil if he healed a person and, in doing so, broke the law? The issue here is especially ambiguous because Jesus' healing on the sabbath, rather than waiting until sundown, would seem to be totally arbitrary: the person has been paralyzed for a long time, and the healing could perfectly well wait until sundown, or so it would seem. And Jesus' questions seem to be beside the point. Jesus asks not only, "Is it lawful to do good or to do harm on the sabbath?" but also, Is it lawful "to save life or to kill?" The latter question appears to assume that *not* to heal—and so to obey the sabbath law— would be to *kill*! From what perspective can Jesus' questions be understood?

Of course, no one would agree that it is lawful to kill; but none of the bystanders would have agreed, either, that saving life, or killing, was at stake on that sabbath in the synagogue. For them what was at stake was whether an act of healing could just as well wait until evening to be performed. Their perception of the scene was very different from Jesus' perception. For them, Jesus' question was irrelevant; for Jesus, their posture was evil. For them, Jesus' alternatives were not the only alternatives—Jesus was putting false questions to them; for Jesus, they did not perceive that the dominion of God was at hand. For Jesus, the moment was to be illumined by the mercy of God. The *present* moment was decisive—not time, or history, not what might be done tomorrow, or next year, but the "Now." The questions Jesus put to the bystanders reveal Jesus' assumptions about the will of God in the present moment, and the meaning of the presence of God's dominion.

Jesus' justification for his act of healing presupposed the correctness of his questions. Were Jesus' questions the right questions? Was Jesus' perception of the world the right perception? The issue in Jesus' mind was not whether the law was valid—Jesus never denied that it was. The relevant issue was, rather, whether the dominion of God had come near, and whether an action based on the perception that it was indeed near, was the right action. Jesus' action assumed the nearness of God's dominion and actualized it. Jesus' questions were in perfect agreement with his perception of the nearness of the dominion of God. When God is present, God does not withhold mercy today simply because there will be time to have mercy tomorrow. The presence of God is a merciful presence, and, from Jesus' point of view, to postpone showing mercy—to withhold life—was "to kill."

The questions one asks depend on one's perception of reality. If God is not assumed to be coming near, or to be present, then one set of questions is appropriate; but if God or God's dominion is assumed to be "at hand," then one asks a different set of questions and one's actions will grow out of them. From Jesus' point of view Jesus' questions were correct, but from the point of view of those seeking to entrap Jesus, they were nonsense.

So Mark says Jesus looked around at the people "with anger." Anger, or anything approaching it, is very seldom attributed to Jesus in the Gospels; and it is interesting to note that both Matthew and Luke omit that observation here (see Matt. 12:12 and Luke 6:10). Both Gospels also fail to follow Mark when Mark says later that Jesus was "indignant" at the disciples' reaction to people who were bringing little children to Jesus.[1] Quite apparently "anger" and "indignation" are not characteristics the Gospel authors wished to attribute to Jesus, and in Matthew Jesus goes so far as to forbid anger in *anyone,* saying that anybody who is "angry" at a brother or sister (that is, probably, another Israelite or another human being) will be liable to judgment (Matt. 5:22).

But the earlier Gospel, Mark's Gospel, says that Jesus looked around at the people with anger, was grieved at their insensitivity, and said to the paralyzed person, "Stretch out your hand." The one with the withered hand stretched it out, and it was restored, cured. Jesus had been angry that malicious, "righteous" human beings were trying to catch him performing an act of mercy on the sabbath. He saw through their hypocrisy and exposed it for what it was. And he performed the cure. It appears that Jesus' fearless behavior in the presence of a Jewish crowd, very much opposed to Jesus and seeking to catch him in a breach of the sabbath law, was an important example to be held up in the Gospels before later disciples.

Mark tells us at the conclusion of this narrative that the Pharisees formed a plot with the Herodians to "kill" Jesus (v. 6). That verse is apparently a later addition to the narrative, for the Gospels do not contain any development of a conspiracy plot against Jesus. But the verse provides a dramatic conclusion to the narrative. Jesus *was* the object of great anger, which was solidified and came to its peak after Jesus' act of mercy on the sabbath.

The Gospels do not represent Jesus as objecting to the law, or as holding that the law was not given by God or was irrelevant to Jewish life. The Gospels do maintain, however, that Jesus, not the law, is Sovereign in the church.

[13]

Jesus' Resurrection

No story about Jesus should conclude with the ending of Jesus' historical life. To do so would be like telling the story of a president of the United States and ending it before the person was elected president. Most New Testament witnesses to Jesus testify to a postcrucifixion Jesus, to "appearances" to those who had known Jesus, and to Jesus' presence with believers in the community of faith after Jesus' death.

The Synoptic Gospels

At the end of the Gospel of Matthew an angel tells Mary Magdalene and "the other Mary" that Jesus "has been raised" (28:6). The women are to tell Jesus' disciples that Jesus "has been raised from the dead," and is going ahead of them "to Galilee" where they "will see Jesus" (Matt. 28:7, Inclusive Version). We should note that Matthew does not describe the resurrection itself. The angel simply told the women that Jesus was not in the tomb, that Jesus had been raised. The resurrection is over; it is a thing of the past. That is always the case wherever Jesus as "raised" is talked about either in the Gospels or Paul: Jesus' "resurrection" is never described; it is assumed. Then Matthew tells us that later, when Jesus met the women, they "took hold of Jesus' feet, and worshiped Jesus" (Matt. 28:9, Inclusive Version).

But the author of Matthew has no interest in discussing the mode of Jesus' appearance, an appearance that had long since taken place when he wrote and would not be repeated. In Matthew Jesus' appearance to the disciples provides the occasion for Jesus to address Jesus' postcrucifixion commission to them and, through them, to the wider church. On the mountain where Jesus commanded the disciples to go, Jesus "speaks" to them (28:18), telling them to "go . . . make disciples" by "baptizing" and "teaching [the new disciples] to obey everything that I have commanded you" (28:19–20). The only thing Matthew says about Jesus' appearance to the disciples, which is minimized, is that they "saw" Jesus (in a *dependent* clause, 28:17). A literal translation of Matt. 28:17–18 would be, "and after seeing Jesus, they worshiped. . . . And Jesus said to them . . ." Matthew's emphasis is not on what the disciples *saw,* but on what Jesus *said.* Jesus' commandments are to be observed, and Jesus promises that the words Jesus spoke earlier, "where two or three are gathered together in my name, I am there among them" (Matt. 18:20), will be fulfilled. Jesus' last words to the disciples are, "Remember, I am with you always, to the end of the age" (28:20). Through the decades and centuries the church will not witness Jesus' appearances, but it will hear Jesus' word.

At the end of his Gospel, Matthew's primary emphasis is on the missionary charge Jesus gives the disciples on the mountain in Galilee. The idea of a universal mission charge (including Gentiles) authorized by Jesus, is late. Nothing of the kind is reflected earlier in the church. In Gal. 2:7 Paul knows nothing about such a charge, and he works out a division of labor with Peter, arguing that his gospel will go to the uncircumcised, and Peter's to the circumcised. But in Acts 10:45 the Jews are amazed that "the Holy Spirit had been poured out even on the Gentiles."

Matthew believes that what Jesus commissions after being raised coincides with what Jesus has said before the crucifixion. The Jesus who speaks to the church after the crucifixion is the same Jesus of Nazareth who spoke in Palestine during his real life; so what Jesus says now is continuous with what Jesus said then. The Gospel of Matthew serves the function of elucidating what the risen Christ commands the church by reporting what Christ said in Palestine, and by repeating what it means to obey Jesus. That the main point of Matthew's resurrection narrative was not to say something about *Jesus*—that Jesus had been raised from the dead and had made some postcrucifixion appearances on earth—is indicated by the fact that Matthew provided no occasion for the *disappearance* of the Jesus whose feet the women had grasped (28:9). Matthew felt no obligation to have Jesus' body evacuated because it was not Jesus' body that Matthew was talking about, but the Jesus who, in possession of all authority in heaven and on earth, is with Jesus' disciples always—in Matthew's church, and to the end of the age. So there is no ascension story in Matthew as in Luke. Jesus simply remains "with" the disciples, "always."

In Mark there is no resurrection narrative at all, as there is also no appearance narrative (see 16:1–8). The Gospel of Mark ends with a "young man" (Mark 16:5), who probably connotes an angel, at Jesus' tomb; and the "young man" tells "Mary Magdalene, and Mary the mother of James, and Salome" that Jesus the "crucified one . . . has been raised" (Mark 16:6, author's translation)—raised, of course, by God. What we refer to as the "resurrection of Jesus" has already taken place. It is announced as over. It is not described. That God has raised Jesus is an article of faith demanded by the fact of Jesus' presence in the church. What we have in Mark is *preaching, undemonstrable kerygma.* And the message is: "Jesus has been raised." Then subsequently, as corroborating evidence for the truth of the proclamation, the "young man" adds, "Look, there is the place they laid the body" (Inclusive Version). The empty tomb is offered as evidence of the reality of the resurrection, which is presupposed.

Mark then tells us that trembling and terror took hold of the women. It is quite clear that neither the proclamation of Jesus' resurrection, nor the corroborating evidence of the empty tomb, created faith in them. The women did not believe when they were told that Jesus had been raised—even when they observed that the tomb was empty. Finally, the women are told to tell the disciples that Jesus is going ahead of them to Galilee, where they will "see Jesus" (16:5–7, Inclusive Version). The "seeing," whether the reference is to Jesus' parousia or to an appearance of Jesus, is not described. Mark simply affirms that the "seeing" will take place.

We must remember, however, that in addition to what Mark says at the end of his Gospel, Mark earlier has included the apocalypse of

Jesus Christ

chapter 13, in which Jesus speaks of " 'the Human One coming in clouds' with great power and glory" (13:26, Inclusive Version). Although the origin, composition, history, and significance for Mark's theology of the "Little Apocalypse" of chapter 13 are all difficult to estimate, it is clear that Mark has included in his Gospel the coming of "the Human One" who will be "seen." Mark also has a reference to the *coming* of "the Human One" in the "glory of God" or "with the clouds of heaven" (Mark 8:38, Inclusive Version; cf. also 14:62). This "coming" is for the purpose either of saving (13:27), or of condemning (8:38). So while Mark has no "resurrection narrative," Mark obviously assumes what we speak of as "Jesus' resurrection." The reality also is that the same may be said for every other New Testament author: no New Testament author describes Jesus' resurrection; but the New Testament authors as a whole all assume it.

In the Gospel of Luke women who had "come with Jesus from Galilee" (23:55, Inclusive Version) visited Jesus' tomb and "did not find the body" (24:3). They were told by "two men in dazzling clothes" that Jesus was not there, "but was raised" (24:5, author's translation). Then the women went and "told this to the apostles" (24:10), but the apostles did not believe the women and thought their words were "an idle tale" (24:11). As in Mark, neither the announcement that Jesus had been "raised," nor the empty tomb, generated faith (cf. Luke 24:2–4, 10–11, 22–24).

Luke then recounts "appearances" of Jesus on three occasions: (1) the appearance to Simon (24:34), reported but not narrated; (2) the appearance to the two disciples on the road to Emmaus, when Jesus walked with them and "went in to stay with them" when they got to their destination. The Jesus who walked with the two disciples was not the historical person they had known, was not even identifiable by them, but had already entered "into [Jesus'] glory" (24:26). And while Jesus and the two disciples were "at the table," Jesus "took bread, blessed and broke it, and gave it to them," and the eyes of the two men were opened, and "they recognized Jesus," who then "vanished from their sight" (24:13–31, Inclusive Version). It was at the Sovereign's table that the "raised" Jesus was identified as the real Jesus who had been crucified. (3) Jesus' third appearance in Luke was to the eleven and others gathered in Jerusalem (24:36–53). The climax of Luke's postcrucifixion narrative is found in the last words Jesus speaks in Luke's Gospel: "You are witnesses of these things. And behold, I am sending upon you the promise of my Father-Mother. You stay in the city until you are clothed with power from heaven" (24:48–49, author's translation). Then Luke says that Jesus "raised Jesus' hands, and blessed them. While blessing them, Jesus parted from them and was carried up into heaven" (24:50b–51, author's translation).

The point of all these so-called "resurrection narratives" of Matthew and Luke is not so much to tell believers something about *Jesus*, although the stories in Matthew and Luke do include some descriptive details about Jesus. But the main point of all these Gospel narratives is to tell their hearers and/or readers something about themselves and the Christian community. Mark ends with the "terror and amazement" of the women after their confrontation with the "young man" in the tomb, but the last word spoken by that "young man" was that the disciples would "see Jesus" in Galilee. Matthew makes it clear that Jesus would be with the disciples "always." That is the culminating statement of the whole Gospel.

In the Gospel of Luke the main point is very similar to Matthew's. The Emmaus story tells believers that Jesus is known in the "breaking of the bread" in the church. The following story tells believers that in the church's Supper it is really *Jesus'* presence that is known. That is the significance of Jesus' words: "Look at my hands and my feet; see that it is I myself. Touch me and see; for a ghost does not have flesh and bones as you see that I have" (Luke 24:39). And that is also the significance of Luke's additional words that when Jesus had said this, "Jesus showed them the hands and the feet . . ." (Luke 24:39–40, Inclusive Version).

Finally, in Jesus' last appearance in Luke's Gospel, Jesus promises to send to the community gathered around Jesus "what my Father-Mother promised," that is, the Spirit (Luke 24:49; Acts 1:4–5). And in the second chapter of Acts Luke describes the fulfillment of that promise in the Pentecost narrative (Acts 2:1ff.).

Jesus Christ

Paul

In Paul's letters it is also the case that all language about Jesus having been "raised" is directed to what that raising means for believers, not to what it meant to Jesus. Early in 1 Corinthians 15 Paul's emphasis in quoting the tradition he had received might appear to be for the purpose of narrating what happened to Jesus after Jesus "died," "was buried," and "was raised" (1 Cor. 15:3–4). But Paul soon makes it clear that his recitation of the tradition regarding events after Jesus was crucified and was raised was not to tell the Corinthian church something about Jesus, but it was to establish the veracity of the only ground of the life and hope of *Christians*: "If Christ has not been raised, then *our proclamation* [that Christ *was* raised from the dead] has been in vain and *your faith has been in vain*" (1 Cor. 15:14). And later in the chapter Paul writes: "If Christ has *not* been raised, *your faith is futile* and you are still in your sins. Then those also who have died in Christ have perished. If for this life only we have hoped in Christ, we are of all people most to be pitied. But in fact Christ has been raised from the dead . . ." (15:17–20a). Paul's preaching that Christ has been raised from the dead is for the purpose of validating his gospel, without which "raising" the faith of believers is without any basis, without any profit, and utterly worthless. Paul's adjectives in this passage are very strong. He is saying emphatically that faith in Jesus cannot exist if Jesus was not raised from the dead, because if Jesus was not raised from the dead, there is no one to believe in. In order to believe, one has to believe *in* someone or something. Like the writers of the Gospels, Paul's statements about Jesus being "raised from the dead" do not have as their primary intention to say something about a postcrucifixion life of Jesus, or about Jesus' experience of life after death.

In 2 Cor. 4:8ff. Paul writes: "We are afflicted in every way, but not crushed; bewildered, but not despairing; persecuted, but not abandoned; struck down, but not destroyed; always carrying in the body the putting to death of Jesus, *so that the life of Jesus may be manifested in our body*" (author's translation). By the "life of Jesus" that is manifested in the present historical life of believers, Paul is not referring only to Jesus' earthly life, but to the life-giving life of that real Jesus, who was raised, and who "appeared" to Paul (1 Cor. 15:8). It is the Jesus to whom Paul referred when writing to the Corinthians, "To the married I give this command—not I *but Christ . . .*" (1 Cor. 7:10, Inclusive Version). The "putting to death of Jesus" in one's understanding of oneself is at the same time one's participation in the life of Jesus who was raised. The "life" is not offered apart from the "putting to death." Similarly, when Paul begged the Sovereign to remove the "thorn" in his flesh, the Sovereign "kept telling" him, "My grace is all you need, for power comes to its full strength in weakness" (2 Cor. 12:7b–9a, author's translation). That grace was the "grace of the Sovereign Jesus Christ, and the love of God."

In 2 Cor. 4:12 Paul goes on to say that "death is at work in us, but life in you." This does not mean that life is not also at work in Paul when he writes, which would contradict v. 10; but it highlights the paradox that the life that is given presupposes the "putting to death." Remember what Paul writes to the Romans: "Do you not know that all of us who have been baptized into Christ Jesus were baptized into Christ's death? Therefore we have been buried with Christ by baptism into death, so that, just as Christ was raised from the dead by the glory of the Father-Mother, so we too might walk in newness of life" (Rom. 6:3–4, Inclusive Version). Also to be especially noted in the Romans passage is the last clause, which says pointedly that the fact that Christ was raised makes it possible for believers to "walk in newness of life." The point of the preaching that Christ was raised from the dead was not to tell of a new experience of Christ, but to open the way for believers to set out on a life that is lived, as Paul says in Rom. 1:17, "from beginning to end in faith" (author's translation).

Paul writes further in 2 Corinthians 4, "We know that the one who raised the Sovereign Jesus will raise us also with Jesus, and will present us as acceptable [same verb in 1 Cor. 8:8, translated in NRSV as 'will bring us close'] together with you"; and all this is to the end that "grace . . . may increase thanksgiving, to the glory of God" (2 Cor. 4:14–15, author's translation). The raising of Christ provides the basis for the raising of believers, and in Christ the entire believing community ("us together with you"), the corporate body of believers, will be acceptable to God. In typical Pauline fashion, Paul concludes that the purpose of the whole saving event is "to increase thanksgiving, to the glory of *God.*"[1]

We should also note Paul's view that it is the earthly life of Jesus, his mission and his sufferings up to and through the cross, that are to characterize the life of Jesus' disciples, whose hope in the resurrection life is based on Jesus' assumed resurrection. The life that is to be manifested "in our body"—that is, communicated by the Spirit, by the presence of the raised Sovereign—is Jesus' "real" life. The Jesus whose life is recorded in the Gospels, and the Jesus who was raised and is present in the community gathered around Jesus, is the same Jesus. It is the New Testament, and only the New Testament, that testifies to who the "real" Jesus *was,* who the Jesus *is* whom the church knows and worships. The two Jesuses are related to each other dialectically, each informing and informed by the other. The church cannot be the church without its scripture, for its scripture tells the church who Jesus is, the Jesus in whom the church sees the face of God. The church's scripture is the church's mooring and its guide.

The Gospel of John

After the death of Lazarus, the author of the Fourth Gospel has Jesus say to Martha, the brother of Lazarus, "I am the resurrection and the life. Those who believe in me, even though they die, will live, and everyone who lives and believes in me will never die" (John 11:25–26). Who is the "I" who speaks here, the "I" who "is" the resurrection and the life? It is the Jesus who acts and speaks in the Gospel of John, who addresses Martha, and it is also the Jesus who acts and speaks in the lives of believers, who addresses the community which "believes" in Jesus, and who, in being "lifted up from the earth, will draw all people" to Jesus' self (John 12:32).

Jesus' resurrection means not only that Jesus is present with believers, that they may "walk in newness of life" (Rom. 6:4), but it also means that believers have grounds for hope in their future with Christ, a future that is also at the same time present.

Jesus' Resurrection

We have noted that it is the same Jesus, whose life and crucifixion are told about in the Gospels, who is also Sovereign in the church. It is the same Jesus, but in a different mode. The Jesus who speaks and acts in the Gospels is not present anymore, and has not been present since Jesus died. So while there is continuity between the historical Jesus and the "raised" Jesus, there is also discontinuity. In fact, in the resurrection narratives of the Gospels, the discontinuity seems more evident than the continuity, partly because, I think, the continuity is taken for granted. Let us look at these narratives for the evidence.

In Matthew 28:1ff. the author says that the women who had gone to the tomb, who had been told by an angel that Jesus was not there but had been "raised," and who were on their way to tell this to the disciples—these women were met by Jesus, who greeted them; and then they "worshiped" Jesus (v. 9). The reference to "worshiping" Jesus (the verb is repeated in v. 17) indicates that this Jesus was not present in the same mode the women had known before the crucifixion, when they had not "worshiped" Jesus. And in the rest of Matthew's narrative it is the *discontinuity* that is most evident. In Matt. 28:5–7 the angel at the tomb tells the women that the Jesus "who was crucified" is "not here," but "has been raised" and is "going ahead" of the disciples to Galilee where they will "see" Jesus. The above narrative about Jesus and the women follows immediately after these words spoken by the angel.

Then later, in Matt. 28:17, we are told that "having seen" Jesus, the eleven disciples also "worshiped" Jesus; "but some doubted." First of all, it is to be noted that Matthew puts the "having seen" in a dependent clause. It is not the "seeing" that Matthew emphasizes, but the "hearing" of what Jesus said (vv. 18–20). And once again, the reference to "worshiping" Jesus indicates discontinuity, some change in the mode of the Jesus whom the disciples "saw" and "heard." But the fact of the "doubting" is a still stronger indication that the Jesus who met the eleven on the mountain in Galilee was no longer the historical figure, but was now the figure whom they worshiped, in whom they had faith as well as doubt.

The Greek that the NRSV translates "but some doubted" is subject to a different translation, and to a quite different meaning from that indicated by the NRSV. The NRSV translation would mean that while the eleven disciples "worshiped" Jesus, some of them (or some others who perhaps were not disciples) "doubted"—that is, they were not convinced by "seeing" Jesus. But the Greek words can be translated differently. Their meaning is more probably that those who worshiped Jesus also "doubted." The more natural translation of the words the NRSV translates "but *some* doubted" would be "but *they* [also] doubted."

The only other place where the word translated "doubted" is found in the whole New Testament occurs in one other verse in Matthew, in words Jesus speaks to Peter (Matt. 14:31). In that narrative Peter asked Jesus to command him to walk to Jesus on the water. And Jesus said, "Come." So Peter began to walk toward Jesus on the water; but when a strong wind came up, Peter became afraid and began to sink, and he cried out to Jesus, "Sovereign, save me!" So Jesus reached out and caught Peter, saying, "You little-faith person, why did you *doubt*?" Peter had faith—he was walking on the water—but he did not have *sufficient* faith. He also doubted, and began to sink. In his doubting he was saved by Jesus. The underside of his faith, we might say, was doubt. And it is quite possible that at the end of Matthew, when the eleven met Jesus in Galilee, and saw Jesus, and worshiped Jesus, and were about to hear Jesus' command to them, they also doubted. Like Peter earlier, they were "little-faith" people; the underside of their faith was doubt. But Jesus *spoke* to them, and said, as the last words in Matthew, "I am with you always, to the end of the age." The Jesus who saves is always present to the disciple who has faith, but is "afraid," and "begins to sink," and "cries out."

When we look at Luke 24 we see again that through most of the end of that chapter, Jesus is not even recognized. Though there is a hint of recognition in the community's "joy" that attends their "unbelief," and their "amazement," Jesus is carried up into heaven before their eyes, and presumably returns to Jesus' glory (see 24:26). Then, as in the Gospel of Matthew, Jesus is "worshiped" (24:52). The real Jesus is "carried up into heaven," but the "raised" Jesus is present in the Spirit, in "power from on high."

In the Gospel of John we see features we are familiar with from other Gospels. In John, as in Luke, the sight of the empty tomb is not interpreted to mean that Jesus has been raised (see 20:1–2). Mary Magdalene surmises that Jesus' body has been stolen (20:2), and she "weeps" because of the theft (v. 11). And the empty tomb has no more meaning to Peter than it had to Mary Magdalene (20:9), so John says that "they did not yet understand that Jesus must be raised" (20:9). Resurrection is not the only possible meaning of the empty tomb. Only the beloved disciple, the ideal believer, interprets the meaning of the empty tomb correctly (20:8)—a meaning that the earliest form of the visit narratives in Luke and the form lying behind John had not incorporated. Only believers understand the meaning of the fact that the tomb was empty.

The fact that Mary Magdalene does not recognize Jesus, but supposes that the person she is speaking to is the gardener (20:14–18), indicates, once again, a change in the mode of the person Jesus, and points to the discontinuity between the real Jesus and the raised Jesus. The visible mode in which Jesus appears to Mary Magdalene is not recognizable. Only when Jesus speaks— when Jesus calls Mary's name—is Jesus recognized. Recall John 10:3: the sheep hear Jesus' voice when Jesus calls Jesus' own by name. The empty tomb speaks of the continuity; the nonrecognition speaks of the change. In John there is not a simple continuity between the Jesus who "goes" to God[2] and the Jesus who "comes" to the disciples[3] after Jesus has "gone." It is the same discontinuity that Paul talks about in 1 Cor. 15:42–44 when he says that what is sown is a "physical" body, but what is raised is a "spiritual" body.

When, in John, Jesus appears to the *disciples* in the evening (20:19ff.), Jesus is the "glorified" Jesus, who gives the Spirit (20:22). Jesus has "come"; and so the condition of 7:39 is fulfilled: "The Spirit was not yet [received] because Jesus had not yet been glorified." When the Spirit is received, Jesus is already glorified.

We note a difference between Jesus' appearance to the disciples in the evening (vv. 19ff.), and Jesus' appearance to Mary Magdalene in the morning (vv. 15ff.) When Jesus appears to Magdalene

Jesus has not yet ascended ("I have not yet ascended to God," v. 17), and is not yet glorified, so Mary does not receive the Spirit; but when Jesus appears to the disciples in the evening Jesus is glorified (cf. 7:39), and so Jesus gives them the Spirit. Apparently, also, when Jesus appears to the disciples Jesus has ascended to God, for it has been implied that Jesus must *go* in order to send the Paraclete, or Spirit (cf. 15:26; 16:7); but in 20:17 Jesus tells Mary Magdalene to go tell the disciples that Jesus *is going* to God (that is, Jesus has not yet gone).

In the Gospel of John the meaning of Jesus' "resurrection" is that Jesus *ascends,* that Jesus "goes" in order to "come" and give the "Spirit." The question as to why Jesus did not continue to appear after Jesus' appearance to the disciples is really a false question. Jesus' appearance to the *disciples* was made to give the Spirit, which is *always available. That* is Jesus "coming." In the book of Acts Jesus *goes* before the Spirit *comes;* but in John, the Spirit *is* Jesus. So John does not have an ascension narrative corresponding to Luke's. From John's theological point of view, resurrection and ascension are a single event that takes place over a period of a week.

This interpretation of the resurrection and ascension is consistent with the rest of John's Gospel. In John 16:7 Jesus says, "It is to your benefit that I go away, for if I do not go away, the Advocate will not come to you; but if I go, I will send [the Advocate] to you." Jesus also promises elsewhere, "If I go . . . I will come again" (14:3); "I am coming again" (14:18); and "we [that is, 'my Father' and I] will come . . . (14:23). In John 20:17 Jesus is ascending to Jesus' "Father," who then becomes the *disciples'* "Father." When the Spirit is given, those who receive the Spirit become "children of God" (3:4, 5).

On the evening of the same day, when Jesus appeared to the disciples, Jesus "breathed" on them and said to them, "Receive the Holy Spirit" (20:22). The "breathing" of Jesus brings to mind God's "breathing" "into the nostrils of the human creature" the "breath of life" (Gen. 2:7). This is the culminating statement of John's postglorification narrative. Faith is now possible: belief in Jesus, authentic life, love for one another—all are now possible. And eternal life has been given to the disciples. The Gospel opened on the theme of creation: "all things came into being through the Word" (John 1:3, Inclusive Version). So the Word, having been made flesh, having come to the world as Life-giver from God, and having returned to God, creates the community around Jesus—the community to which eternal life is given, which lives by and from the Spirit, or Jesus. The giving of the Spirit is John's Pentecost, which happens, in John, on Easter, which is also the time of the parousia.

Epilogue

This book is not a "life of Jesus." It does not attempt to be a biography of the person who lived in Palestine two thousand years ago, in whose life Christians have found theirs; nor is it written for the person who is expert in New Testament studies. This book is written, rather, to broaden the spectrum through which pastors and lay people may read particularly the Synoptic Gospels (Matthew, Mark, and Luke) more intelligently, and allow them to speak with new clarity and relevance.

Today Christians are more and more disclosing a vital interest in listening more carefully to the voices that created and have sustained the church. Believers who take their faith seriously, and who desire to investigate the roots of their faith and to learn more about who it is who is at the center of their faith, are turning to the text of their Gospels in increasing numbers, wishing to make contact with what they can know about Jesus. But they are discovering that they cannot read the Gospels the way they read other literature—that the Gospels are not self-explanatory, and that one needs some technical guidance and illumination if one is to begin to penetrate the mystery of their substance.

So in the first three chapters of this book the reader is exposed to a range of issues that arise as soon as one engages in the serious study of the Gospels. In the first place, one must deal with the implications of the fact that the four Gospels, not to mention the extant noncanonical gospels, provide the reader with multiple testimonies about who the historical person Jesus was. What are the

Epilogue

implications for the believer of the existence in our canon of such a great variety of witnesses?

Second, there is the fact that the Synoptic Gospels contain a number of different sources that came into existence over a period of some fifty or sixty years. How accurately can one date these sources, and what is the significance for faith of the fact that some sources are earlier than others?

Third, there is the interesting situation created by the fact that the Gospels were written long before there were printing presses, and we do not have a single Gospel, or any biblical book for that matter, as it came from the hands of its author. What we have are handwritten copies of earlier handwritten copies of what was written—more than five thousand copies in all of the New Testament or parts of it. And, as one would expect, no two copies are exactly the same; in some cases they are very different, so one must make judgments about which reading probably comes closest to what one supposes was originally written. Are there any rules that are applicable in making such judgments? What one reads in any English translation of the New Testament always represents judgments of the translator(s) about which reading from which manuscripts most probably represents the original Greek text.

This brings us to the matter of translation. The Gospels, like the whole New Testament, were written in Greek, not English. When one reads an English translation of a Gospel one is not reading what was written in Greek by the author of the Gospel in the first century C.E., but one is reading a translation of copies of what was written. Differences in English translations often represent the fact the translator(s) have made different judgments about which readings are probably the better ones; but sometimes they represent different judgments about how to translate the same Greek words. These various issues, all of them important in reading the Gospels, are taken up and discussed early in the book.

There is also another, broader matter involved in reading the Gospels, and that is what is known as "hermeneutics." Hermeneutics is the way by which one moves from a "there" of a text or art

Epilogue

form, to a "here." In the case of literature, it is the way by which one comes to an understanding of what one is reading. In order to understand anything that is written, one must make some judgment about the kind of literature it represents, and then make some further judgment about the way in which that particular writing is to be understood. For example, if one is reading a telephone book, one will ask only questions that are appropriate to it. A telephone book will make a specific kind of sense, so one will ask of it only limited kinds of questions. If, on the other hand, one is reading a chemistry textbook, one will read it in a different way. Reading a novel requires its own way of reading; reading a poem, still another way—the mind will work differently in each case. Hermeneutics analyzes the way by which any literature is to be read and understood, as well as the way by which any art form is to be appropriated and interpreted.

When one reads a Gospel, in order to interpret it, one must ask of it questions that are appropriate: What kind of literature is this? Is the language "steno" language that speaks precisely and is to be interpreted literally, or is it "tensive" language that communicates in a very different way? Or is it both? Precisely what kind of language is it, and how does this language work? How does one get from that ancient literature to one's own contemporary world? These questions, combined with what Jesus meant by the specific expression "dominion of God," occupy the central part of this book.

Most scholars agree that the "dominion of God" (or, "kingdom of God") constituted a major emphasis in the preaching of Jesus—perhaps it was Jesus' primary concern. What images came to Jesus' mind when he thought about it? What images came to the minds of his hearers? What did the term connote? What does the term connote today to believers in the church? To discuss these issues a hermeneutics is required, and this book then moves to that discussion. The hermeneutics of Rudolf Bultmann, a most influential New Testament scholar of this century, is discussed, and then the book moves on to lengthy expositions, relevant to hermeneutics, of what a metaphor is; of what an image is; of how mythological language, and signs, and symbols work. A separate chapter deals with manifestations of the dominion of God in the Gospel of Mark.

Epilogue

The heart of this book centers on one aspect of the teaching and preaching of Jesus: the dominion of God. Aside from a brief discussion of the relationship in Jesus' mind of the dominion of God to the Jewish law, the book does not raise any of Jesus' other words for discussion. So it is neither a "life of Jesus," nor a survey of what Jesus taught and preached. Its scope is far more modest.

Finally, the central event in Jesus' life and the central event in the Christian faith—the crucifixion—is not discussed in this book at all. The reason is that elaboration of the history and meaning of Jesus' crucifixion would require its own volume. No one doubts that Jesus' crucifixion took place; that it happened is assumed. And the essentials of *what* happened are known; it is the *why* of the crucifixion that requires inquiry and interpretation. The resurrection, however, is a different matter. Paul did not need to write to any church that "if Christ was not *crucified,* our preaching is in vain and your faith is in vain." No one questioned that Jesus had been crucified. But Paul did write to the Corinthians that "if Christ has not *been raised,* our preaching is in vain and your faith is in vain." As narrated in the New Testament, the raising of Jesus from the dead does not center on an experience of Jesus. No one is told anything about what the raising of Jesus meant to Jesus. As narrated in the New Testament, the resurrection is about an act of God that discloses Jesus' presence to Jesus' disciples. The last chapter of this book talks about the ways in which the authors of the Gospels do this.

NOTES

PREFACE

1. Luke Timothy Johnson, *The Real Jesus* (San Francisco: HarperSan-Francisco, 1996), v.
2. Robert W. Funk and Roy W. Hoover, *The Five Gospels* (New York: Macmillan Publishing Co., 1993), 5.

1. MULTIPLE TESTIMONIES

1. Burton H. Throckmorton, Jr., *The New Testament and Mythology* (Philadelphia: Westminster Press, 1959), 212–13.
2. Quoted in J. B. Bury, *The Idea of Progress* (London: Macmillan & Co., 1920), 338.
3. Quoted in Karl Löwith, *Meaning in History* (Chicago: University of Chicago Press, 1949), 97f.
4. Charles Baudelaire, *Diary of a Writer,* August 1880, quoted by Löwith, 98.
5. In *Tolstoi's Flucht und Tod,* ed. F. Fulop-Miller and F. Eckstein (Berlin, 1925), 103. Quoted in Löwith, 99.
6. Julius Wellhausen, *Einleitung in die drei ersten Evangelien* (Berlin: Reimer, 1906).
7. Wilhelm Wrede, *The Messianic Secret,* trans. J.C.G. Greig (London and Cambridge: James Clarke, 1971). German original *Das Messiasgeheimnis in den Evangelien* (Göttingen: Vandenhoeck & Ruprecht, 1901).
8. Karl Ludwig Schmidt, *Der Rahmen der Geschichte Jesu* (Berlin: Trowitzsch & Sohn, 1919).
9. See Ernst Käsemann, "The Problem of the Historical Jesus," *Essays on New Testament Themes* (London: SCM Press, 1960), 15–47.
10. N. T. Wright, *Who Was Jesus?* (Grand Rapids: Wm. B. Eerdmans Publishing Co., 1992), 12.

Notes

11. See Preface, n. 2.
12. Morton Smith, *Jesus the Magician* (San Francisco: Harper & Row, 1978).
13. John M. Allegro, "Jesus and Qumran: The Dead Sea Scrolls," in *Jesus in History and Myth,* ed. R. J. Hoffman and G. A. Larue (Buffalo, N.Y.: Prometheus Books, 1986).
14. Geza Vermes, *Jesus the Jew* (London: William Collins Sons & Co., 1973). See also *The Religion of Jesus the Jew* (Minneapolis: Fortress Press, 1993).
15. Bruce Chilton, *A Galilee Rabbi and His Bible: Jesus' Use of the Interpreted Scripture of His Time* (Wilmington, Del.: Michael Glazier, 1984).
16. S.G.F. Brandon, *Jesus and the Zealots* (New York: Charles Scribner's Sons, 1967).
17. John Dominic Crossan, *The Historical Jesus: The Life of a Mediterranean Jewish Peasant* (San Francisco: HarperSanFrancisco, 1991). See also Burton L. Mack, *A Myth of Innocence: Mark and Christian Origins* (Philadelphia: Fortress Press, 1988); also Mack's *The Lost Gospel: The Book of Q and Christian Origins* (San Francisco: HarperSanFrancisco, 1993), and Mack's *Who Wrote the New Testament? The Making of the Christian Myth,* ibid., 1995).
18. Bruce Barton, *The Man Nobody Knows: A Discovery of the Real Jesus* (Indianapolis: Bobbs-Merrill Co., 1925).
19. Bob Briner, *Management Methods of Jesus* (Nashville: Thomas Nelson Publishers, 1996).
20. Quotation from *The New Testament and Psalms: An Inclusive Version* (New York: Oxford University Press, 1995).
21. See Ernst Käsemann, "The Canon of the New Testament and the Unity of the Church," *Essays on New Testament Themes,* 95–107.
22. Martin Luther, *Lectures on Romans* in *Library of Christian Classics,* 15, trans. and ed. by Wilhelm Pauck (Philadelphia: Westminster Press, 1961), 196f.

2. DIFFICULTIES IN DISCOVERING JESUS

1. Luke Timothy Johnson, *The Real Jesus,* 144.

Notes

3. GOSPEL SOURCES AND TEXTS

1. See, for example, Burton H. Throckmorton, Jr., *Gospel Parallels,* 5th ed. (Nashville: Thomas Nelson Publishers, 1992).

4. THE DOMINION OF GOD

1. See, for example, E. P. Sanders, *Jesus and Judaism* (Philadelphia: Fortress Press, 1985); also Maurice Casey, *From Jewish Prophet to Gentile God: The Origins and Development of New Testament Christology* (Louisville, Ky.: Westminster John Knox Press, 1991).
2. German original, *Der Christliche Glaube,* 1821, 2d ed., 1830. English trans. ed. by H. R. Mackintosh and J. S. Stewart, 1928.
3. Published in French as *La Vie de Jésus,* 1863; English trans., 1888.
4. Ernest Renan, *The Life of Jesus,* People's Edition (London: Temple Co., 1888).
5. Maurice Goguel, *The Life of Jesus,* trans. Olive Wyon (New York: Macmillan Co., 1933), 51.
6. Ernest Renan, *Life of Jesus,* 83.
7. See Bruno Bauer, *Kritik der Evangelien und Geschichte ihres Ursprungs* (Berlin: Gustav Hempel, 1850–52).
8. English trans. of *Die Predigt Jesu vom Reiches Gottes* (Göttingen: Vandenhoeck & Ruprecht, 1892).
9. I am indebted for the following discussion to the work of Norman Perrin, *The Kingdom of God in the Teaching of Jesus* (Philadelphia: Westminster Press, 1963), 17ff.
10. The Assumption of Moses, trans. R. H. Charles and rev. J.M.P. Sweet, in H.F.D. Sparks, ed., *The Apocryphal Old Testament* (Oxford: Clarendon Press, 1984), 612f., revised also by author.
11. Quoted by Rudolf Bultmann, *Jesus Christ and Mythology* (New York: Charles Scribner's Sons, 1958), 13.

5. THE HERMENEUTICS OF RUDOLF BULTMANN

1. Rudolf Bultmann, *Glauben und Verstehen,* vol. 2 (Tübingen: J.C.B Mohr [Paul Siebeck], 1933), 211–35.

Notes

7. METAPHOR

1. See Susan B. Thistlethwaite, "On the Trinity," *Interpretation* 45, no. 2 (April 1991): 159–71.
2. See Mary Rose D'Angelo, "Abba and 'Father': Imperial Theology and the Jesus Tradition," *Journal of Biblical Literature* III, no. 4 (winter 1992): 611–30.
3. Denise Levertov, *Mass for the Day of St. Thomas Didymus* (Concord, N.H.: Wm. B. Ewert, 1981).
4. *Collected Poems of T. S. Eliot* (New York: Harcourt, Brace & Co., 1936), 214.
5. An anecdote from Alan W. Watts, retold in Philip Wheelwright, *Metaphor and Reality* (Bloomington, Ind.: Indiana University Press, 1962), 155–56.

8. SIGNS, IMAGES, AND SYMBOLS

1. See chap. 7, n. 5, passim.
2. Paul Tillich, *Systematic Theology,* vols. 1–3. (Chicago: University of Chicago Press, 1951–63).
3. Percy Bysshe Shelley, "To Night," in *The Poetical Works of Percy Bysshe Shelley,* ed. Edward Dowden (London: Macmillan & Co., 1895), 569.
4. From A. E. Housman, "White in the Moon," in *English Literature and Its Backgrounds,* Shorter Edition (New York: Dryden Press, 1930), 1271.
5. Wheelwright, *Metaphor and Reality,* 92.
6. Wallace Stevens, "Man Carrying Thing," *The Collected Works of Wallace Stevens* (New York: Alfred A. Knopf, 1954), 350.
7. William Ralph Inge, *Christian Mysticism* (New York: Charles Scribner's Sons, 1933), 5.
8. Ibid., 250.

9. MYTH, SYMBOL, AND DOMINION OF GOD

1. See chap. 5.
2. Wheelwright, *Metaphor and Reality,* 130.
3. See Norman Perrin, *The New Testament: An Introduction* (New York: Harcourt Brace Jovanovich, 1974), 21–33.

Notes

4. See chap. 3, n. 1.
5. *Inclusive Language Lectionary,* Rev. Ed., Year B (Atlanta: John Knox Press, 1987), 18. See also discussion in chap. 4.
6. *Inclusive Language Lectionary,* Rev. Ed., Good Friday, Years A, B, C.
7. Suggested to me by a student.

10. SIGNS IN MARK OF THE DOMINION OF GOD

1. Origen, *Contra Celsum* 8.58.
2. Martin Noth, *Leviticus* (Philadelphia: Westminster Press, 1977), 114.
3. G.A.F. Knight, *Leviticus* (Philadelphia: Westminster Press, 1981), 83.

11. THE DOMINION OF GOD TODAY

1. Marge Piercy, *The Twelve-Spoked Wheel of Flashing* (New York: Alfred A. Knopf, 1978), 31–32.

12. JESUS AND THE LAW

1. See Mark 10:14 and the parallels in Matt. 19:14 and Luke 18:16.

13. JESUS' RESURRECTION

1. See 2 Cor. 4:15; also Rom. 15:6–9a; 1 Cor. 10:31; Phil. 1:11; 2:11.
2. See John 13:3; 14:12, 28; 16:5, 10, 17, 28, etc.
3. See John 14:3, 23, etc.

INDEX OF BIBLICAL REFERENCES

OLD TESTAMENT

Genesis

2:7   130

Exodus

20:8ff.   108

Leviticus

15:1   97
15:19ff.   97
15:25ff.   97
24:5–9   111–12
24:8   29

Numbers

28:9–10   29, 114

1 Samuel

21:16   29, 112, 114

2 Samuel

22:50   94

Nehemiah

10:30ff.   107

Psalms

5:1   93
103:13   70
137:1   65
145:11–13   84

Isaiah

40:1–2   87
40:10   48, 86

41:2b   86
45:1–2   86
53:4–5   87
60:12a   87

Jeremiah

1:10   101

Hosea

6:6   30, 114–15

Zechariah

14:9   48–49

OLD TESTAMENT
APOCRYPHA

Assumption of Moses

10:1–10   47

NEW TESTAMENT

Matthew

2:1–12   31
2:1–20   31
2:13–16   31
3:13–17   28
4:23   36
5:19   85
5:20   84
5:22   118
5:39–42a   8
5:44   8
6:9   8
6:9–13   33, 38
6:10   49, 85
7:9–10   37

7:29   1
8:5–13   90
8:11   85
11:11   85
12:1–8   28–29, 113–15
12:5–7   29
12:6   30
12:9–14   115–18
12:22–29   90
12:25ff.   89
12:25–29   47
12:28   96
12:41–42   31
13:43   42
14:31   128
16:18   32
18:1   32
18:3   84
18:15–35   32
18:15   35
18:23–35   31
19:17   85
19:29   88
20:1–16   31
21:28–32   31
22:2–14   89
24:37–39a   48
25:1–13   31
25:34   88
26:26   34
26:29   42
27:16–17   38
27:46   34
28:1–7   127
28:6–9, 17–20   120

Index of Biblical References

28:17–20	127	7:1–10	90	16:7	130
28:20b	101	10:25	88	20:1–2	129
		10:29–37	31	20:7	130
Mark		11:2–4	33	20:9	129
1:7	48	11:2	85	20:14–18	129
1:9–11	28	11:11–12	37	20:15ff.	129
1:15	43	11:20	49	20:17	130
1:21	26	11:31–32	31	20:19ff.	129
1:39	36	12:13–21	31	20:22	129, 130
1:40–44	90	12:32	49		
2:27	29, 112	12:50	86–87	**Acts**	
2:22–28	107, 111	14:13, 15–24	89	1:4–5	123
2:23–28	28–29	15:11–32	31	2:1ff.	123
2:23	29	17:26–27	48		
2:25	29	18:9–14	31	**Romans**	
2:26	29	18:18	88	1:17	125
2:27	12	22:19	34	2:29	16
2:28	12	23:34	35	6:3–4	125
3:1–6	115–18	23:43	35	6:4	126
5:22–24	35–42	23:55	122		
5:25–34	96	24:2–4, 10–11,		**1 Corinthians**	
5:25–34	90	22–24	122	2:14–15	16
8:12	82	24:13–31	122	7:10	125
8:38	122	24:26	122	11:2	25
9:43	85	24:36–53	123	15:3	25
9:47	84–85	24:39	123	15:3–4	124
10:17	88	24:48–49	123	15:8	125
10:23	85	24:49	123	15:14	124
10:35ff.	86,87			15:42–44	129
10:42–45	87	**John**			
13:24–25	60–61	1:1, 14	ix	**2 Corinthians**	
13:26, 27	122	1:3	131	3:6	16
14:22	34	1:14	40	4:8ff.	124–25
14:36	86	3:4, 5	130	4:12	125
15:34	34	4:10	ix	4:14–15	125
16:1–8	121	6:33	ix	12:7b–9a	125
		7:39	129, 130		
Luke		10:3	129	**Philippians**	
1:46–56	31	14:3	130	2:6–7	40
2:1–20	31	14:18	130		
3:21–22	28	14:23	130	**1 Thessalonians**	
4:44	37	12:32	126	1:9–10	24
6:1–5	28–29	7:39	129		
6:6–11	115–18	11:25–26	126		

INDEX OF NAMES

Allegro, John M., 138
Aristotle, 68

Barton, Bruce, 11, 138
Baudelaire, Charles, 6, 137
Bauer, Bruno, 45, 139
Brandon, S.G.F., 138
Briner, Bob, 11, 138
Bultmann, Rudolf, 15, 53–58, 65, 81, 139
Bury, J. B., 137
Burckhardt, Jakob C., 6

Casey, Maurice, 139
Chilton, Bruce, 138
Crossan, John Dominic, 138

D'Angelo, Mary Rose, 140
Debs, Eugene V., 11
Descartes, René, 74
Dostoevsky, Fyodor, 6

Eliot, T. S., 72, 140

Flaubert, Gustave, 6
Funk, Robert W., x, 8, 137

Goguel, Maurice, 139

Housman, A. E., 75, 140

Inge, William Ralph, 78–79, 140

Johnson, Luke Timothy, x, 22, 137, 138, 144

Kaftan, Julius, 30
Käsemann, Ernst, 8, 137, 138
Kierkegaard, Søren, 6
Knight, G. A. F., 141

Lessing, G. H., 4
Levertov, Denise, 71, 140
Löwith, Karl, 137
Luther, Martin, 17, 138

Mack, Burton L., 138

Nietzsche, Friedrich, 6
Noth, Martin, 141

Origen, 96, 141

Perrin, Norman, 139, 140
Piercy, Marge, 103–4, 141

Reimarus, H. S., 4, 44
Renan, Ernest, 45, 139
Ritschl, Albrecht, 5, 44–48

Sanders, E. P., 139
Schleiermacher, Friedrich, 44
Schmidt, Karl Ludwig, 7, 137
Schweitzer, Albert, 10, 50
Shelly, Percy Bysshe, 75, 140
Smith, Morton, 138
Spencer, Herbert, 5
Stein, Gertrude, 80
Stevens, Wallace, 75–76, 140

Tatian, 4, 16

Index of Names

Thistlethwaite, Susan B., 140
Throckmorton, Burton H., 3, 139
Tillich, Paul, 22, 74, 140
Tolstoy, Leo, 6, 137

Vermes, Geza, 138

Watts, Alan W., 140
Weiss, Johannes, 46–51, 53–54
Wellhausen, Julius, 6, 137
Wheelwright, Philip, 73, 76, 81, 140
Wrede, Wilhelm, 7, 137
Wright, N. T., 8, 137